Untangling the Mess

Revealing the Certainty of God's Love

Pam Northrup

This book is dedicated to all those who have been told that they need to do something or change something before God will love them.

CONTENTS

Impassioned Clay

Deep in ourselves resides the religious impulse.

Out of the passions of our clay it rises.

We have religion when we stop deluding ourselves that we are self-sufficient, self-sustaining, or self-derived.

We have religion when we hold some hope beyond the present, some self-respect beyond our failures.

We have religion when our hearts are capable of leaping up at beauty, when our nerves are edged by some dream in our heart.

We have religion when we have an abiding gratitude for all that we have received.

We have religion when we look upon people with all their failings and still find in them good; when we look beyond people to the grandeur in nature and to the purpose in our own heart.

We have religion when we have done all that we can, and then in confidence entrust ourselves to the life that is larger than ourselves.[1]

Richard N. Helverson

---

[1] Richard N. Helverson, *Singing the Living Tradition*, (Boston: Unitarian Universalist Association, 1993), 654.

INTRODUCTION

This book is a labor of love. It is born out of my love for God and my love for humanity. I'm especially motivated by love and respect for people hurt by organized religion and those seeking a new or renewed relationship with God. I hope that my words will shed new light on who God is and how much God loves you. Thank you for joining me as we seek to untangle the mess that's been made of God's love so that we can see more clearly God's abundant love.

In my work as a pastor and hospice chaplain, I have opportunities to converse with people of a variety of faiths and people who claim no faith or religious affiliation at all. It's a privilege to hear people share how their faith impacts their lives. I appreciate the honesty and courage it takes for people to admit that believing in God or belonging to a church isn't relevant to them. Verbalizing how you think or don't think about God is an increasingly tricky disclosure when everyone around you believes that Christianity is the only way to live.

I've heard beautiful accounts of how a person's faith got them through some tough times and how their faith community cared for them along the way. I give thanks for these examples of how a person's faith and their faith community can be a source of peace and blessing to them. They reveal the best of what affiliation with a faith community is all about. I sincerely wish that every faith community would be a place of acceptance, understanding, and life-giving relationships.

Unfortunately, faith communities don't always function at their best. People have told me heartbreaking stories about being excluded from a faith community because of who they are, who they love, what they've done or not done. I've cried with people who've shared stories about the various ways "church-going" people have pushed them away because they didn't fit with their established expectation of a "good" church member.

We create a tangled mess of God's love by using hurtful and manipulative tactics to scare people into denying who they are, changing their ways, or accepting Jesus. We rob people of an encounter with the Holy when our biblical interpretations and religious practices make things too complicated. Using the Bible or church policy to exclude, limit, hurt, or manipulate another person creates a knot. Each of these knots need to be untangled so that the certainty of God's love is revealed in all its abundance, authenticity, beauty, and simplicity.

One Sunday morning in the congregation where I served as pastor, I noticed a mother and her daughter sitting in the pew. They were first-time worshippers with us. When it came time for Holy Communion, the mom got up and took her daughter to the bathroom rather than coming forward to receive communion. They returned to the service for the last hymn and then left quickly.

Several weeks later, the mother and her daughter returned. They came in after worship started and left after the final hymn, so I wasn't able to speak with them. Several more weeks went by before they came back. This time they arrived before the service, and we were able to talk with each other. As we talked, I learned more about them and what was drawing them to worship.

During the conversation, I gently explained that they were both invited to receive Holy Communion during the service. Mom seemed surprised and told me that this was not what our bulletin indicated. She pointed to the printed explanation about communion and the statement that said, "Baptized Christians may receive Holy Communion." She said, "we're not baptized," then went on to say that sitting in the pews while others communed was uncomfortable, so that's why they stepped out of worship.

I felt horrible and apologized for making her feel uncomfortable. I thanked her for continuing to come to worship and stressed that, despite what the bulletin said, she and her daughter were welcome to commune whenever they attended worship. They chose not to commune at worship that Sunday but chatted with me after the service. Mom requested an appointment with me so they could learn more about the congregation, receiving communion, and being baptized.

My heart broke for this mom and her daughter, and for the way our messaging had inadvertently made them feel unwelcome. They mustered the courage to walk into a church for worship but then couldn't fully participate because they had not fulfilled a required prerequisite. Still, they kept coming back.

As I thought about what happened, I realized how uninviting the practice of limiting communion to only the baptized was. The reality is, I don't check the baptismal records of anyone who comes to communion, so how would I know who was baptized and who was not. The practice of requiring baptism before receiving communion doesn't reflect my understanding that Holy Communion is not something we need to earn. Instead, it is a gift from God, a tangible and loving way of experiencing God.

Rather than make communion contingent on being baptized, can we make space for God to work through the receiving of Holy Communion to draw someone to baptism? After explaining what happened to the lay leaders in the congregation and my theological thoughts on the matter, we decided to modify the invitation so that all worshippers were welcome to receive Holy Communion.

When I met with the mom and her daughter a week or so later, I answered their questions about communion and baptism. I encouraged them to receive Holy Communion the next time they were in worship. It was a joy to watch them come forward with big smiles and outstretched hands several weeks later.

Our communion practices created a tangled mess. They restricted someone's full participation in worship and made them feel excluded from the community. We didn't want that to happen, but it did. Thankfully both mother and daughter continued to attend worship and, in so doing, revealed a knot that needed untangling so that all were truly welcome.

I intend to untangle the mess that's been created so everyone can know and experience the abundance and certainty of God's love. It's a love given unconditionally by God. It doesn't depend on what you say and do or what you don't do or don't say. God's love embraces you just as you are and longs for you to enjoy the blessings that come through that love.

I hope that in reading this book, you will encounter a different way of thinking about God and God's relationship with you. By reframing some long-held ways of thinking about God, this book will highlight the significance of God's blessings, which flow from the heart of God and are yours because God loves you.

Part one of this book identifies and unties five common knots formed when:

- "God Said It. I Believe It. That Settles It." is how the Bible is understood

- God's love is dependent on what we say or do

- a narrow view of God limits our ability to see the bigness of who God is and the vastness of how God can be experienced

- there is an overemphasis on brokenness

- theological understandings create obstacles to experiencing the certainty of God's love.

In part two, the quilt of God's love is assembled from the untangled threads revealing that God's love is:

- already given to you

- extravagant, encompassing, and empowering

- based on acceptance, not rejection; compassion, not cold-heartedness; inclusion, not exclusion; and peace, not despair

- filled with the blessings of joy, comfort, strength, hope, interconnectedness, and courage

- supported by living with intention, humility, and balance and embracing paradox, mystery, yourself and others, and spiritual practices that nourish you.

Don't worry! I don't intend to convert you to a set of specific beliefs or compel you to become part of a particular faith community. Instead, I want this book to bring healing from the harm or pain caused by the tangled knots which have caused some to employ hurtful tactics and manipulative messages about who God is and what God expects from you. I want you to be wrapped in the comfort of God's loving embrace which cherishes your uniqueness and celebrates your goodness.

Some explanations before we get any further:

- I believe that you are loved by God already; therefore, I will refer to you as beloved throughout the book.

- I believe that God is not bound by gender. I've chosen to avoid using pronouns altogether, rather than using male pronouns for God. This may seem awkward at first. I hope that it won't be a distraction or frustration for you. At times, I'll refer to God by other names.

May you be blessed by the reading of this book, and may the love of the Divine enfold you in peace and hope this day and forevermore.

Pam Northrup
April 2020

PART ONE

Untangling the Knots

*One of the main tasks of theology is to find words
that do not divide but unite, that do not create
conflict, but unity, that do not hurt but heal.*

Henri Nouwen

CHAPTER 1

The Knot of "God Said It. I Believe It. That Settles It."

Receive the text as a gift that keeps accumulating meaning. For in so doing, you may find it has much more to do with directing your life in love than in serving as a prop to support your favorite interests.

Peter Marty

The problem with this knot

You've probably heard someone say: "God said it. I believe it. That settles it." This saying sums up the typical way that the knot of Biblical Fundamentalism is understood.

Peter Marty defines Biblical Fundamentalism as "that impulse to interpret the scriptures in a rigid way, fixating on the presumed literal and factual accuracy of every verse within the Bible."[2] This way of thinking about the Bible is based on the claim that the Bible is inerrant, without error, and infallible, without fault. Approaching the Bible, this way assumes that every word of scripture was given directly by God, so how it appears in the Bible is correct. Biblical Fundamentalism sees the Bible as God's only and final word, therefore what the Bible says settles it.

Biblical Fundamentalism leads to a narrow interpretation of scripture. For some, applying a literal understanding of the Bible reduces confusion because the reader accepts what's printed on the page just as it is. Biblical fundamentalism is over-simplistic and problematic. This way of approaching the Bible fails to appreciate that God continues to speak to us in new ways every day.

Untying the knot

This knot is untied by embracing the following principles about the Bible:

---

[2] Peter Marty. *The Anatomy of Grace,* (Minneapolis, MN: Augsburg Fortress, 2008), 24

First, the Bible is inspired

The Bible was written by men who believed that they were inspired by the Holy Spirit to tell their experiences of God, creation, and humanity. No one walked around taking dictation as the story of God enfolded. Before the stories were written down, they were shared orally. Imagine our faithful ancestors sitting around the fire when someone asks, "How did we get here?" or "Who is the Lord you keep speaking about?" I suspect that the responses were unique to each storyteller because God interacted with people in ways that were meaningful to them. When the elders and keepers of the stories died, their stories were written down. Often it was decades, and sometimes centuries, after the events took place. This doesn't mean that the memories were wrong; they were just different. Holding on to all of them gives us the fullness of the story.

The writers wrote from the heart, remembering the stories they'd been told, and sharing the unique ways that God interacted with people and communities. At places, the words of the Bible are confusing, and at other places, they seem to contradict each other. Sometimes they seem incomplete because there are gaps in the story. That's what happens when you take 66 distinct writings and put them together in one volume. When we think about the Bible as inspired, we embrace the nuances rather than let them cause us to question the Bible's validity. This sets us free to approach each book, chapter, and verse with our eyes and heart wide open to see what God has done, is doing, and promises yet to do.

Second, the Bible is to be interpreted.

Every translator, commentary writer, reader, listener, student, teacher, and preacher interprets the Bible. Interpretation happens when we try to make sense of what's happening at the moment by thinking about what we see and hear. Anytime you are reading or studying the Bible, it's helpful to acknowledge what is influencing your interpretation, your understanding. Questions like: What experiences am I bringing to the reading of scripture? What messages have I heard or read that are impacting my understanding? What is my motivation for reading the passage? What do I hope to get out of this reading? Asking these and other questions guide how you interpret and read the Bible.

Every reader and interpreter of scripture brings their own experiences, cultural background, and historical understandings to the task of encountering the written scriptures. That's why different people can read the same passage and draw different conclusions. That's why you can come to a particular understanding one day and a different interpretation another day. Recognizing this opens up the text to allow the reader to go deeper into the scriptures, see the nuances as a blessing, become comfortable asking tough questions of the passage, and be enriched by the encounter with the Bible every time.

We can apply different methods for reading and interpreting scripture; each provides a unique perspective. A historical lens pays attention to the author, setting, audience, and wonders how social and cultural context influenced the writer. A literary lens focuses on how the genre and what comes before and after the passage you're reading. A devotional focus invites the reader to identify the word or phrase that speaks to them and then reflect on what God is saying to them in that word. When applying a theological lens, the reader looks to their religious tradition and spiritual understandings to shape their interpretation of the passage. They ask questions and engage in conversation with the text by looking for insights that shape how they are responding to the reading. While these lenses can be applied independently of each other, using them together gives us a complete understanding of a particular passage.

Next, the Bible is God's love story.

The main character in the Bible is God. Everyone else is a participant in God's story because everything in the Bible starts and ends with God. Between the pages of the Bible, the extent that God goes to show love to all unfolds. God's love shows forth at creation; continues through the history of the Israelites, kings, and prophets; is made known in the life, death, and resurrection of Jesus; is manifested in the writings of Paul and the early Christian church, and is revealed once again in a glimpse of the restored creation through the vision of John.

The Bible is one way we are encountered by the Word of God, but it's not the only way. God's Word also meets us through Jesus, who is God's Word in the flesh (John 1). God's Word encounters us through preaching, singing, looking at a beautiful sunset, feeling the ebb and flow of the ocean, and in the raindrops falling from the sky. God's Word encounters us in the face of a newborn baby, the cashier at a grocery store, and the stranger on the street. When we acknowledge the Bible as one way, among many, that God's Word encounters us, we are set free to experience God in a wide variety of ways. Each one unfolds more and more about who God is and who we are in relationship with God, creation, and each other.

Finally, the Bible is a book of faith.

One day while in my church office, I received a call from someone wanting to know if we believed in the Bible. The conversation went like this:

I said, "no," and then explained, "we read from the Bible every week in worship, but we don't believe in it. Our belief is in God. We believe that the Bible tells us about God, Jesus, and the Holy Spirit. It tells us the stories about our faithful ancestors, the prophets, and the disciples. It describes the extent God goes to show love to us."

Astonished, the caller said, "Then how can you be a Christian church?"

I explained, "The Bible is central to our worship because it shows us who God is. We read and study the Bible to help us know God better. I'd love for you to come to worship so that we can talk more about this."

"Well, I can't come to your church if you don't believe in the Bible," the caller responded and then hung up.

While believing in the Bible may seem like something Christians are supposed to do, it's not. Worshipping or believing in the Bible, turns the Bible into an idol that can come between God and us. When the words of the Bible become more important than an encounter with the living God, revealed through scripture and in other ways, we've lost our way.

The Bible is a book of faith. It's written to proclaim who God is and how God interacts with creation. It's written to draw us closer to the Holy. The Bible is not a history or science book. The Bible doesn't predict the future or give us a way to anticipate the second coming. The Bible doesn't identify who's in and who's out, who's right and who's wrong. It doesn't tell us which decisions to make and how to move through life. The Bible is not the complete and infallible story of God, because God's story continues unfolding every day. Instead, the Bible is our book of faith that shows us who God is and who we are in relationship with God and one another.

<u>Questions to ponder</u>

- What did you hear or learn about the Bible as you were growing up?

- What place, if any, does the Bible have in your life now?

- If you read the Bible, what approach do you use?

- What questions or concerns do you have about the Bible?

CHAPTER 2

The Knot of Making God's Love Dependent on Us

The Christian does not think God will love us because we are good, but that God will make us good because he [God] loves us.[3]

C.S. Lewis

I t was a warm spring afternoon when I attended the memorial service for the mother of a friend at a local funeral home. I found a place to sit that was about halfway to the front and on a side aisle in case I needed to leave before the service was over. But, as more and more people arrived, I

---

3 C. S. Lewis, *Mere Christianity*, (New York: HarperCollins, 2001), 63.

ended up in the middle of a long pew, surrounded by strangers.

The funeral went as expected. Because my friend's mother loved her pastor, the family invited him to officiate at the service. They provided him an outline of how they wanted the service to go and expected him to follow the plan. At first, the observance went as expected. There were comments from family members about how much they loved their mom and how much she loved them. A granddaughter read a poem which she wrote in memory of her grandmother. We listened to a couple of recorded hymns, played through the sound system, while family photos appeared on the screen. The preacher read several Bible passages and then preached a rather lengthy sermon. Near the end of the sermon, the preacher addressed the survivors and the rest of us with these words:

"I visited with your mom many times before she died. She often shared how concerned she was about your salvation because she didn't want to be separated from you in heaven."

I thought, *Really. You're going to go there right now in the middle of the service. Their mom is at rest. She's fine. Don't lay this crap on them!*

Sadly, this preacher didn't know the mourners sitting in front of him. He didn't know their stories, nor did he understand that their spiritual life was a source of pain that caused their relationship with their mother to unravel. My friend told me that religion was one thing they agreed not to talk about. So, here we are at their mom's memorial service.

He continued, "Your mom made me promise that I would stress how important it was to her that you accept Jesus as your Lord right now. She doesn't want this funeral to end without you being able to accept Jesus into your heart. Because you loved your mother, I'm sure you want to do this for her so that she can spend eternity in peace."

Oh, my goodness! I thought. *I can't believe that you're using these tactics to guilt this grieving family into keeping their mom at peace. Don't you know that coerced and forced love isn't love at all!*

If I wasn't trapped in the middle of a pew, I would have walked out. But no, I was stuck.

The officiant continued, "So, we're all going to close our eyes. Then I'll pray a short prayer and ask that you repeat the words after me so that Jesus can come into your heart. Your mom will be so pleased that you're doing this today. Let's pray."

This "short" prayer went on for quite a while. I looked around the sanctuary and saw a room full of people, also with their eyes open, squirming uncomfortably in their seats. The officiant called the adult children by name in the prayer and stressed to the Lord, on their behalf, how sorry they were for everything they'd done wrong. Finally, after reminding us to repeat after him, he included the sentence that I dreaded,

"Lord, I love you and want you to come into my heart today."

The entire time this prayer was rambling on, my anger burned within me. How dare this preacher speak to this grieving family like this. How dare he guilt the survivors into thinking that their mom's peace depends on them accepting Jesus. How dare he use what should have been a celebration of life to bully and provoke the mourners into doing something they didn't choose to do. How dare he take advantage of their grief and vulnerability to berate them for a supposed lack of faith. My heart broke for this grieving family, and the rest of us who suffered through this together.

After the prayer, the preacher smiled at us and concluded, "Because you have asked Jesus into your heart today, your mom will be at peace, and someday, if you follow the commandments and live like Jesus wants you to, you'll be reunited with her."

Oh no, I thought. *This can't be happening. You manipulated my friend, her family, and the rest of us into a moment to accept Jesus, and now you're making our relationships with Jesus dependent on what we do. You've declared that their mom's okay, but we're still in jeopardy. Oh my.*

The service finally ended, and everyone exited the chapel. There were many people in attendance so I couldn't check in with my friend until the next day.

When I asked her what she thought of her mom's service, she said, "I hated it! I'm so embarrassed that my friends, family, and co-workers had to sit through something like that. What did he think he was doing?"

Before I could respond, she continued, "Why did he think it was okay to hijack my mom's service and turn it into something that we didn't want? We worked hard to plan a beautiful celebration of mom's life, which he ignored and instead imposed his own agenda. I'm so angry and disappointed. I can't believe that mom really wanted him to behave like that. I hope I never see that guy again!"

I shared my friend's anger and disappointment. Memorial services and funerals are hard enough without having a pastor, someone you'd expect to be compassionate and kind, throw religion in your face, and use the death of your loved one as an opportunity to badger you.

In some denominations of the Christian church, people must prove that they are a "real" Christian by giving an exact date for when they accepted Jesus. My oldest daughter was an active leader of a Christian group in her high school. The summer between her junior and senior years, a new faculty advisor took over the group. She decided to interview all of the leaders to make sure that everyone was a "true" Christian. When my daughter went to her interview, the advisor asked for the date she accepted Jesus as her Lord. My daughter replied, "Jesus accepted me when he died on the cross." The advisor answered, "that's nice, but you still need to accept Jesus, or you can't be a leader." My daughter stood up and walked out of the room. Unfortunately, many of the other student leaders did the same. I was furious. This advisor not only impacted an essential social activity for my daughter and others at her high school, but she also questioned the legitimacy of my daughter's faith. Her actions were hurtful and manipulative.

The problem with this knot

These hurtful tactics and manipulative messages only turn people off, generating unhealthy feelings like fear, shame, anger, and guilt. These feelings, in turn, drive unintended actions. The recipients of these messages may choose to turn away from all aspects of organized religion. They may vow never to step foot into a church again or may throw their hands into the air asserting that none of it matters anyway.

The experience that my daughter had and the experience of my friend at her mother's funeral are inappropriate. They make God's love and acceptance dependant on something that a person does or says. My friend needed to ask Jesus into her heart in order to give her mother peace in heaven. The advisor made my daughter's acceptance as a leader in the Christian organization, dependent on her having an exact date for when she accepted Jesus as her Savior. Both approaches make people angry and cause them to say, "if this is what being a Christian is all about, I want nothing to do with it!"

Untying the knot

Maybe you've been on the receiving end of hurtful and manipulative messages. Messages like:

- you have to accept Jesus before you can go to heaven

- you'll go to hell if you die before you've asked Jesus to come into your life

- you have to be baptized before you are saved

- you must attend worship, read your Bible, pray, and tithe to show how faithful you are.

Maybe these messages have caused you to wonder and question: Have I been good enough to get into heaven? Does God love me even though I've done (fill in the blank)? What if I've not been to church in a while, or never read the Bible, or don't pray, will God still love me? What if I've never accepted Jesus as my Savior?

These messages may come from friends and family members, a preacher or evangelist, or an assortment of Bible verses quoted by a concerned Christian who believes that it's their responsibility to save you. I suspect that they don't mean to cause you harm or pain. Some might say that they are following the command of Jesus, who said, "[19]Go therefore and make disciples of all nations, baptizing them in the name of the Father and of the Son and of the Holy Spirit, [20]and teaching them to obey everything that I have commanded you. (Matthew 28).

These words of Jesus are important and do shape how Christian congregations understand their place in their communities. What concerns me is how Christians live out this call. Do our actions manipulate, threaten, and bully people into becoming a follower of Jesus? Do our words and actions make people feel unloved and unlovable? Do our messages cause people to question their self-worth, their dignity? I certainly hope not.

Instead of saying and doing things that cause people to turn away from religion, and maybe even God, our lives need to reflect the love and acceptance that God shows us. Rather than manipulate others, let's embrace them. Rather than threaten others, let's extend hospitality. Rather than bully people, let's walk with them. This is how the knot is untied.

Beloved, when well-meaning Christians tell you that God's love for you depends on your actions, your choices, and your thoughts, they are misrepresenting God's love. God's love doesn't rely on you. It is unconditional, steadfast, and nonnegotiable. This love starts and ends with God, and God already loves you.

Questions to ponder

- What are the messages you've heard about God's relationship with you?

- How have these messages made you feel?

- What are your experiences with a faith community?

- Have you ever been told that you don't belong or that God won't love you unless you do something first? What did that feel like?

- What does it feel like to read that "God already loves you?"

CHAPTER 3

The Knot of a Narrow Understanding of God

Our first task in approaching another people, another culture, another religion is to take off our shoes, for the place we are approaching is holy.[4]

Max Warren, adapted

The problem with this knot

Human beings can be terrified of what they don't understand. While this applies to many aspects of life like history, science, politics, and the economy, it is especially

---

[4] Max Warren, *Lifting Our Voices: Readings in the Living Tradition*, (Boston: Unitarian Universalist Association, 2015), 214.

true when we think about religion and the intersection of faith and life. Our fears cause us to jump to conclusions and form opinions that aren't rooted in truth and understanding. Anxiety can cause us to push people away who don't look like us, love like us, live like us, worship like us, or believe like us.

Our fear leads us to a narrow understanding of who God is and how God relates to the world. We like it when things fit together neatly and when they quickly make sense, including how we think about God and our particular brand of religion or denomination. Many find comfort in what they know and understand. We like it when we can sing the hymns we know, worship the way we've always done it, and pray the Lord's Prayer just as we've done since our childhood. It's nice to feel comfortable. The problem is that feeling comfortable makes it harder to accept change and appreciate differences. It can even cause us to cling more tightly to what is familiar.

Holding a narrow understanding of God and how God relates to us and then protecting that understanding creates an us/them way of thinking. If I'm right about God, then you must be wrong. If my way of understanding God means that I'm in, then you must be out. This way of thinking builds walls that limit our ability to acknowledge and appreciate that God relates to humanity in a wide variety of surprising ways.

Untying the knot

I enjoy talking with people who claim no religious affiliation. In these conversations, people teach me the different ways that they experience the Holy in everyday life. Activities like meditation, yoga, singing, dancing, reading, praying, and walking a labyrinth create space for the Divine to break into our lives. Spending time in nature, with people you enjoy, and around animals are ways to nurture our spirituality. Through these conversations, I've come to understand that even though a person may claim no religious affiliation, they may certainly have a rich spiritual life. One that is not restrained by organized religion. These conversations expand my vision of how God encounters people. They reveal the fullness of God and the expansive ways that God interacts with us all.

I strive to provide spiritual care and emotional support in ways that honor each person's unique expression or non-expression of faith. Sometimes, I offer prayer and readings from the Bible. Sometimes, I read poems or selections from other books. Sometimes, I read the lyrics of hymns or sing familiar songs. Sometimes, we share in conversation about what's happening that day. Either way, the other person shapes how we spend our time together. I appreciate this quote from Jean Rowe because it reminds us of the wide path we travel and calls us to walk with others in ways that are life-giving.

We have a calling in this world: We are called to honor diversity, to respect differences with dignity, and to challenge those who would forbid it. We are people of a wide path. Let us be wide in affection and go our way in peace.[5.]

A story

While preparing to be a pastor, I completed an internship at a local hospital. It was an eleven-week program called Clinical Pastoral Education or CPE. One night while doing a 24-hour shift, I was called to the lobby of the hospital. When I arrived, two women were huddled in the corner, crying. I introduced myself as the hospital chaplain and asked how I could care for them.

The woman told me her husband was dying in the ICU and asked if I would pray for him and them as they waited. She also asked if I was a Christian. I said "yes" and then assured her that I care for people of all faiths and those with no faith at all.

She said, matter-of-factly, "Oh, good. We're Wiccan."

I replied, "Wonderful, I'd like to learn more. Will you tell me what being Wiccan is all about?"

---

[5] Jean M. Rowe, *Lifting Our Voices: Readings in the Living Tradition*, (Boston: Unitarian Universalist Association, 2015), 235.

She explained that they see the Goddess everywhere but especially in nature.

I indicated that I, too, see God in nature and give thanks to God as the Creator of all things.

At that, she relaxed. We talked a bit about her husband, their life together, why he was hospitalized and now dying. After a while, she asked me to pray for them.

Before I began, I asked her to tell me how they address the Holy One and what they believe happens after someone dies, so I could pray for them more specifically.

She said, "You, are the first Christian I've met who is actually interested in learning more about following Wicca. Thank you. You can address the Goddess as Creator. Our path is about celebrating creation and the elements of Earth, Air, Fire, Water, and Spirit. We believe that death is a transition to another realm of existence and that relationships endure beyond death. Please pray that his transition will be peaceful and that he will be at rest."

I thanked her for her explanation and then invited them into prayer. The women embraced me after the prayer and then headed back to the ICU. I received a page to the ICU not long after our time together. When I got there, the man's wife approached me and said, "Thank you for your prayer and understanding. My husband has made the transition, and all is well. Your support meant so much to us!"

I expressed my condolences and thanked them for giving me the opportunity to care for them. We embraced again and then they headed on their way. This was a holy experience for me and one that I continue to treasure. Learning about the path of Wicca and interacting with these two women didn't challenge my Christian faith; instead, it helped me see a bigger view of how the Holy One interacts with the world.

Another story

It has been my privilege to participate in an Interfaith Ministerial Group comprised of a local Jewish Rabbi from the conservative branch of Judaism; a Muslim Imam from the local Mosque; and pastors from the nearby Roman Catholic, Baptist, Methodist, Presbyterian, non-denominational, and Lutheran congregations. We gather several times a year for mutual support, updates on the activities of our faith communities, and exploration of what is happening in our local community and how we can work together to care for our neighbors. Each year, this group sponsors an Interfaith Thanksgiving worship service. Christians, Muslims, and Jews come together to give thanks for God's blessings.

We rotate where the service is held each year, providing us and our parishioners opportunities to be in each other's worship environments. It's important for each faith leader to have a part in the service so the Rabbi offers greetings and reads several passages from the Torah, the Imam also offers greetings and reads several passages from the Quran, and the priest and pastors share readings from the Bible. An assortment of prayers from the different traditions give thanks for the blessings of God.

One year, I was invited to be the preacher. Because Christians, Muslims, and Jews are People of the Book, that is the Bible, I chose Psalm 23 as my preaching text. The Psalm describes the very personal and intimate relationship between the Shepherd and the sheep, between the Creator and the created. Being able to proclaim the Lord's presence, provision, protection, and promise in a sanctuary where Catholics, Protestants, Jews, and Muslims gathered to give thanks was a powerful experience. Together we affirmed and gave thanks for the God who loves us all and doesn't distinguish between who receives the presence, provision, protection, and promise of the Holy One based on their religious upbringing or tradition. We are all included in the net of this love because the Lord is our Shepherd.

This service and the interactions with people of different faiths and denominational expressions reveal to us an expansive God who meets people where they are and whose embrace is wide enough to enfold us all in love. We don't need to emphasize what is different between us. That's simply not helpful and doesn't lead to understanding. Instead, we are set free to look for how we are similar and what we share, letting that build a foundation for relationship and understanding that is based in acceptance rather than tolerance.

It's time to untie the knot of a narrow understanding of God. When we do, we avoid building walls that separate the different perceptions of God or distinctive religious expressions. Let's open our hearts and minds to the experiences of others without judging them. Let's avoid negative talk and thoughts about people of other faiths or no faith. Let's embrace a broader understanding of God which gives us opportunities to meet people where they are and give thanks for the goodness of everyone. A more extensive perception of God enables us to celebrate the things we share, understand how we differ, and honor the unique ways that God meets each of us.

<u>Questions to ponder</u>

- What is your experience with God?

- Where and how do you experience the Holy?

- What is your experience with people of different religious traditions or those who claim no religious affiliation? How has these experiences impacted you?

- What questions, concerns, or insights do you have about this chapter?

CHAPTER 4

The Knot of an Overemphasis on Brokenness

When we live into our original blessing, we renounce the endless fighting stance of original sin and choose instead to live with God. We choose to remember that God surrounds us and sits with us. We remember that God's relationship to us is not in question. We live in blessing, which overrides even our own rebellion against God.

Danielle Shroyer[6]

Original Sin is a dominant doctrine that drives how most of the Christian church thinks about sin and the nature

---

[6] Danielle Shroyer, *Original Blessing: Putting Sin in Its Rightful Place*, (Minneapolis: Fortress Press, 2016), 36.

of humanity. This doctrine teaches that humanity is inherently sinful and promotes a solution based on the acceptance of Jesus, confession of sins, seeking forgiveness, and being baptized. The doctrine of Original Sin overemphasizes the brokenness of our world and the brokenness of humanity. It stresses humanity's separation and distance from God. It makes our relationship with God contingent on what we do and say, therefore shifting the focus away from God to us.

To understand where this knot came from, we need a history lesson

It all goes back to Adam and Eve and the fruit from the forbidden tree. The story goes like this: After God finished creating Heaven and Earth, and after God rested on the seventh day, God created the man and the woman and placed them in the Garden. God provided for Adam and Eve and filled the Garden with fruit trees. They were allowed to eat from the trees, except for the one in the middle of the Garden. A crafty snake is blamed for tricking Eve and Adam into eating the fruit on the forbidden tree. When they ate the fruit of this tree, the eyes of Adam and Eve opened, and they knew that they were naked. Because they disobeyed the Lord and gained the knowledge of good and evil, Adam and Eve were cast out of the Garden.

Since the time of St. Irenaeus and St. Augustine of Hippo, some theologians have taught that the sin of Adam and Eve became the sin for all generations, including unborn children. Irenaeus thought that Adam and Eve's disobedience was because they didn't know better, that they were acting more like children. Augustine thought that their actions were the result of a conscious decision to do what they wanted to do.

Augustine recognized the actions of Adam and Eve as the first time that humanity chose to disobey God. In so doing, they demonstrated that they can make decisions for themselves. Over time, this way of understanding the relationship of sin and humanity became known as Original Sin, a doctrine that describes humanity as inherently sinful from the moment of conception.

Martin Luther and other Protestant reformers challenged a wide range of teachings in the Catholic Church, which caused chaos and confusion. So, to refute the assertions made by these reformers and to reassert Catholic teachings, Pope Paul III convened The Council of Trent (1545–1563). During this Council, the notion of Original Sin became an official doctrine of Catholicism.

Martin Luther accepted the doctrine of Original Sin, and it became part of his understanding of the relationship between God and humanity. Over time Luther became troubled by the way this doctrine was used by the Church to torment the people and pressure them into buying indulgences to mitigate the impact of sin. Reading Paul's letter to the Romans, Luther's theology made a critical shift. Yes, Luther believed that humanity was inherently sinful, but rather than needing to buy an indulgence to save yourself from purgatory, Luther was grasped by Paul's writing, in Romans 3:

> For there is no distinction, [23] since all have sinned and fall short of the glory of God; [24] they are now justified by his grace as a gift, through the redemption that is in Christ Jesus, [25] whom God put forward as a sacrifice of atonement by his blood, effective through faith.

This realization shifted Luther's focus away from the inherently sinful nature of humanity to the abundant grace of God. It caused Luther to formulate the paradox of people being simultaneously saint and sinner. Yes, all have sinned and yes, all are justified by his grace. This way of thinking is one of the things that Luther wanted to debate in his 95 Theses.

Yet despite Luther's efforts, over time, the doctrine of Original Sin seeped into the teachings of the churches of the Reformation. This led some denominations to put a greater emphasis on accepting Jesus as your personal Lord and Savior before a person is made right with God. Baptism was seen as a way to erase the effects of Original Sin. The doctrine of Original Sin continues to influence modern religion today.

The problem with this knot

This doctrine is problematic for me. It doesn't make sense when you look in the eyes of a newborn baby, or hear the laughter of children as they play, or the grief of parents who are burying their child. It doesn't make sense when you sit at the bedside of someone who is dying or around the dining room table as parents try to understand what is happening with their teenager. It doesn't make sense when a person receives a cancer diagnosis or hears that a loved one has died in a terrible accident.

The question at the heart of this is: Why would the Creator call the created being "very good" and then reshape them into an inherently sinful human being? Could it be that the sin of Adam and Eve came about, not because they were inherently sinful but because they were not perfect creations?

God created human beings, with the ability to think about things, experience emotions, make decisions, and take actions. God did this in hopes that the created being would choose to love the Creator and choose to live in a relationship with the Creator and the rest of creation so all would live in unity and harmony. Giving humanity these gifts was a risk that the Creator was willing to take because forced love, forced obedience, isn't love at all.

Because people are not perfect creations, they make decisions and take actions that can harm themselves or others. Because they are not perfect creations, their bodies get sick and die.

Because they are not perfect creations, marriages unravel, people hurt others, accidents happen, and neighbors are neglected. None of this is related to humanity being inherently sinful; instead, it's about not being perfect.

When we start from the place of humanity being inherently sinful, we overlook the uniqueness and beauty of each created individual. We look at each other with suspicion and draw lines between us. Too often, we try to make ourselves look better by putting down someone else. When God's relationship with us starts with people being inherently sinful, we think that God's story is all about us. Taking a negative view of humanity by focusing on sinfulness causes feelings of unworthiness and anxiety. It can eventually push people away from God. This way of thinking leads us to believe that a response from us is necessary to make things right with God.

Now don't get me wrong here. I don't deny that sin and brokenness exist in the world. People continue to exercise their will in ways that cause harm to creation, themselves, and each other. But I no longer accept that people are inherently sinful. God created people in love and bestowed blessings upon them time and time again. I can't imagine that the Creator who creates in love would build in an inherent flaw into the character of humanity.

Yes, Adam and Eve exercised their will and disobeyed the Creator. That decision was born out of pride and the desire to be in charge of their own lives. This action had consequences, but did not forever change the character of humanity. When God created humanity, God declared us "very good," not perfect.

Because we aren't perfect, we will continue to struggle with living in a relationship with creation, ourselves, each other, and God. Our lives will be full of joy and sorrow, peace and anxiety, hope and despair, love, and hate. As we ride this roller coaster of life, we can trust that God is with us because of God's blessing and love.

Untying the knot

It's time to untie the knot that over-emphasizes brokenness and disobedience. Rather than letting Original Sin be the dominant way we think about the connection between God and humanity, let's shift our focus to Original Blessing.

From the beginning, God blessed the new creation with God's presence. God blessed and equipped humanity with emotions and the desire to be in a relationship with others; the ability to think, make choices, and solve problems; and the willingness to learn new things and use our unique gifts and skills to care for others and make a difference. When things went wrong, God continued to extend blessing upon blessing to the people. God released them from captivity, gave them a new homeland, protected them from enemies, and gave them parameters that established how to live in relationship with God and each other. Despite their failures to live faithfully, to love God rightly, God remained in a relationship with them.

Yes, the Lord got angry. Yes, the people experienced the consequences of their disobedience. Yes, the Lord withdrew from the people, but not for long. In time, the Lord extended the blessings of mercy and grace, offered forgiveness, established covenants, and made promises.

God's blessings continued in the person of Jesus. His story is in the four Gospels of the New Testament. Jesus embodied the blessings of God. Jesus turned everything the leaders and people thought they knew about the Holy One and how the world was supposed to work upside down. Jesus loved those others perceived as unlovable, acknowledged those others ignored, and touched those others thought were untouchable. Because his descriptions of a new reality where the lowly are uplifted up, the hungry are fed, the naked are clothed, and the prisoners are set free put him at odds with the religious and political leaders of his day and his parables, miracles, teachings, actions, and interactions turned everything they knew about life and their religious tradition upside down, he was betrayed, arrested, condemned, and crucified.

I've often wondered why God didn't stop what was happening to Jesus. Couldn't the Creator have pulled Jesus out of this terrible predicament or implemented a new plan that didn't include the death of Jesus?

Over the years, I've come to see the actions of God in not rescuing Jesus from what was happening to him as one of God's greatest blessings. You see, God did implement a new plan, did rescue Jesus, not from the cross, but the tomb so that the blessings of God could burst forth and embrace us all.

Beloved, God continues to bless creation with life in the face of uncertainty, health in the face of illness, meaningful relationships in the face of hostility, opportunities to use our gifts and passions to make a difference in our lives as well as the lives of others. God blesses us with freedom from anxiety about what happens at the end of life. Because of God's extravagant, encompassing, and empowering love, we can live full and happy lives in this life and the next.

When we focus on the blessings of God and the many ways that God pursues and shows love to us, we are more likely to see God at work in our lives and the lives of others. Embracing God's Original Blessing empowers us to live in harmony with creation, ourselves, each other, and the Divine. Because of God's blessings, when we stumble (and we will), God says. "I love you," when we build walls between the Divine and us, God says, "I love you," when we wander down different paths, God says, "I love you." In life and in death, we can rest in the assurance that nothing we do, nothing we say, separates us from the love of God (Romans 8:38-39) because God's blessings are already and always upon you and me.

Questions to ponder

- How has your experience of God been influenced by the notion of Original Sin?

- Rather than letting sin dominate the narrative, Pam focuses on the blessings of God throughout the Biblical narrative. What's your reaction to this new understanding?

- How have the blessings of God touched your life already?

- What questions, concerns, or insights do you have about this chapter?

CHAPTER 5

The Knot of Theological Understandings that Create Obstacles

---

*Our huffing and puffing to impress God, our
scrambling for brownie points, our thrashing about
trying to fix ourselves while hiding our pettiness and
wallowing in guilt are nauseating to God and are
a flat-out denial of the gospel of grace.*

Brennan Manning[7]

---

[7] Brennan Manning, *The Ragamuffin Gospel*, (Sisters, OR: Multnomah Publishers, 1990). 18.

The problem with this knot

We often hear we must have faith in Jesus, must believe in Jesus to be saved. This understanding sets up a way of thinking that makes God's love contingent on what we do and say. Paul writes a lot about faith in his letters to the newly developing churches and faith communities. For Paul, having faith is not about a belief in doctrines; it's about trusting—resting—in Jesus who has reconciled us to God.

What the scriptures actually teach

The Gospels of Matthew and Luke include accounts about the birth of Jesus. The Gospel of Mark ignores the birth of Jesus altogether.

> *[14] And the Word became flesh and lived among us, and we have seen his glory, the glory as of a father's only son, full of grace and truth. [15] John testified to him and cried out, "This was he of whom I said, 'He who comes after me ranks ahead of me because he was before me. [16] From his fullness we have all received, grace upon grace. [17] The law indeed was given through Moses; grace and truth came through Jesus Christ. [18] No one has ever seen God. It is God the only Son, who is close to the Father's heart, who has made him known"'* (John 1).

This passage from the Gospel of John stresses the relationship between Jesus and God from the very beginning. Instead of an account about the who, what, and when of the birth of Jesus, we are told that the Word, which was present at creation, now became flesh and lived among us. This Word made flesh is Jesus. In these power-packed verses, we meet Jesus who is "full of grace and truth." We're told that "from his fullness we have all received grace upon grace," reminding us that the law was given through Moses and that "grace and truth" come through Jesus. Jesus, the Word made flesh, is how we know who God is.

Grace, as it is used here, is not about giving thanks for a meal, as in saying grace. Instead, grace is about the unmerited favor of God. It is the unconditional, unearned love of God. Grace comes to us because of who God is, not because of what we do or say. If grace is dependent on us, it wouldn't be grace at all. Jesus is God's unconditional love, he makes that love, that grace, known to humanity through his life, death, and resurrection.

One of the most often quoted verses of the Bible is John 3:16. It's so well known, that people can share it by simply holding up a sign with that citation. But John 3:16 is not enough. The next verse communicates a powerful message:

16 For God so loved the world that he gave his only Son, so that everyone who believes in him may not perish but may have eternal *life. ¹⁷Indeed, God did not send the Son into the world to condemn the world, but in order that the world might be saved through him.*

John 3:17 succinctly summarizes God's motivation in coming down in Jesus, "not to condemn the world, but in order that the world might be saved through him." In this way, grace upon grace is lived out in the person of Jesus.

After his resurrection, Jesus appeared to his disciples, saying, "Peace be with you." He showed them his pierced hands and feet and then as Luke records in chapter 24, he said to them:

> *⁴⁴These are my words that I spoke to you while I was still with you—that everything written about me in the law of Moses, the prophets, and the psalms must be fulfilled.' ⁴⁵Then he opened their minds to understand the scriptures, ⁴⁶and he said to them, 'Thus it is written, that the Messiah is to suffer and to rise from the dead on the third day, ⁴⁷and that repentance and forgiveness of sins is to be proclaimed in his name to all nations, beginning from Jerusalem. ⁴⁸You are witnesses of these things.*

Beloved, the resurrection changed everything! Let me say that again, the resurrection changed everything! When Jesus told the disciples to announce that repentance and forgiveness of sins was to be proclaimed in his name, he was announcing a new reality. A reality that has come about because he has been raised from the dead.

Before his resurrection, the gospel writers depicted the life and ministry of Jesus as one shaped by modeling how to live faithfully with one another and with the Lord. Through his teachings and demonstrations, Jesus hoped that the people would respond, turn away from their unfaithful ways of living, and return to the Lord. This is what repentance is all about.

But the people didn't respond the way that Jesus, the Word, made flesh hoped for. Instead, they protected their ways of being in the world and plotted against Jesus. God recognized that the people couldn't live faithfully on their own. They couldn't believe, couldn't repent, couldn't seek forgiveness because they were focused on themselves, on pursuing their own wants and needs. So, God responded in extravagant love by raising Jesus from the dead, thereby creating a new reality where repentance and forgiveness of sins is already a reality! We no longer need to ask for forgiveness or declare our repentance. These are God's gifts to us and for us.

Fifty days after Jesus was raised from the dead, the Bible tells us that he ascended back to God. Before he did this, he promised that God's presence would be manifested once more in the person of the Holy Spirit. The Holy Spirit would be God's ongoing presence in the world. This presence of God comforts humanity as we experience the ups and downs of life. The Spirit intercedes when we don't know how to pray. The Spirit nurtures us with love, joy, hope, peace, patience, kindness, generosity, faithfulness, gentleness, and self-control. It's the Spirit who draws us close to God and who helps us trust God more fully.

Untying the knot

> [17] *So if anyone is in Christ, there is a new creation: everything old has passed away; see, everything has become new!* [18] *All this is from God, who reconciled us to himself through Christ, and has given us the ministry of reconciliation;* [19] *that is, in Christ God was reconciling the world to himself, not counting their trespasses against them, and entrusting the message of reconciliation to us.* [20] *So we are ambassadors for Christ, since God is making his appeal through us; we entreat you on behalf of Christ, be reconciled to God.* [21] *For our sake he made him to be sin who knew no sin, so that in him we might become the righteousness of God (2 Corinthians 5).*

Notice that "in Christ God reconciled the world to himself without counting their trespasses against them." Therefore, our faith is not required before God loves us. God loves us already! Rather than making faith about us, this passage from Galatians 3 makes faith about Jesus.

> [23] *"Now before faith came, we were imprisoned and guarded under the law until faith would be revealed.* [24] *Therefore the law was our disciplinarian until Christ came, so that we might be justified by faith.* [25] *But now that faith has come, we are no longer subject to a*

disciplinarian [26]*for in Christ Jesus you are all children of God through faith."*

One of the important messages of this passage is that Jesus is faith. Paul says, "Now before faith came" and "until Christ came" to make the case that Jesus is faith. Let's back up a little. God gave the law in love to the Israelites to show them the right way to live in relationship with God and with each other. This provided instruction and protection until "faith would be revealed." Paul tells us that the law was "our disciplinarian until Christ came." All of this was "so that we might be justified by faith."

Continuing in Galatians 3, Paul writes, [25] "But now that faith has come, we are no longer subject to a disciplinarian [26]for in Christ Jesus you are all children of God through faith."

Beloved, now that faith has come, now that Jesus has come, we are no longer subject to a disciplinarian. We are no longer imprisoned and guarded under the Law. Instead we "are all children of God through faith," we are children of God through Jesus who Is faith. It is the faith of Jesus, the only faithful one, that God deems as righteousness.

Romans 5 informs much of my understanding of the relationship between God, Jesus, the Holy Spirit and the gifts that flow from it. The next Bible passages in this section are all from Romans, the 5th chapter.

¹Therefore, since we are justified by faith, we have peace with God through our Lord Jesus Christ, ²through whom we have obtained access to this grace in which we stand; and we boast in our hope of sharing the glory of God. ³And not only that, but we also boast in our sufferings, knowing that suffering produces endurance, ⁴and endurance produces character, and character produces hope, ⁵and hope does not disappoint us, because God's love has been poured into our hearts through the Holy Spirit that has been given to us.

We are justified, made right with God, by faith, that is by Jesus. This justification gives us peace with God and access to grace. God's love, poured into our hearts through the gift of the Holy Spirit, is what enables us to endure suffering, grow in character, and live in hope which, as Paul writes, will not disappoint us.

⁶For while we were still weak, at the right time Christ died for the ungodly. ⁷Indeed, rarely will anyone die for a righteous person— though perhaps for a good person someone might actually dare to die. ⁸But God proves his love for us in that while we still were sinners Christ died for us. ⁹Much more surely then, now that we have been justified by his blood, will we be saved through him from the wrath of God. ¹⁰For if while we were enemies, we were reconciled to God through the death of his Son, much more surely, having been reconciled, will we be saved by his life. ¹¹But more than that, we even boast in God through our Lord Jesus Christ, through whom we have now received reconciliation.

The above verses are some of the most comforting in understanding God's action in Jesus. "While we were still weak," and "while we were enemies," we were reconciled to God through Jesus. This is how God proves the depth of divine love for us. And now that we've been justified, already justified, without a profession of faith, without an acknowledgment of sin, without repentance, we are justified through the actions of Jesus. This justification, this reconciliation, is what saves us, not anything we say or do.

> *[12]Therefore, just as sin came into the world through one man, and death came through sin, and so death spread to all because all have sinned— [13]sin was indeed in the world before the law, but sin is not reckoned when there is no law. [14]Yet death exercised dominion from Adam to Moses, even over those whose sins were not like the transgression of Adam, who is a type of the one who was to come.*

Without the Law, the people didn't know that they were living wrongly. Adam and Eve transgressed against God by thinking that they were superior to God, that they could exercise their will to their own benefit. This led to the expulsion from the Garden. God didn't forget about Adam and Eve but continued to provide for and love them. Once the Law was given by God, as a guardian for the people, the people recognized that the breaking of the Law was sinful.

15But the free gift is not like the trespass. For if the many died through the one man's trespass, much more surely have the grace of God and the free gift in the grace of the one man, Jesus Christ, abounded for the many. 16And the free gift is not like the effect of the one man's sin. For the judgment following one trespass brought condemnation, but the free gift following many trespasses brings justification. 17If, because of the one man's trespass, death exercised dominion through that one, much more surely will those who receive the abundance of grace and the free gift of righteousness exercise dominion in life through the one man, Jesus Christ.

18Therefore just as one man's trespass led to condemnation for all, so one man's act of righteousness leads to justification and life for all. 19For just as by the one man's disobedience the many were made sinners, so by the one man's obedience the many will be made righteous. 20But law came in, with the result that the trespass multiplied; but where sin increased, grace abounded all the more, 21so that, just as sin exercised dominion in death, so grace might also exercise dominion through justification leading to eternal life through Jesus Christ our Lord.

The "one man's trespass" and "the one man's sin" mentioned several times above is a reference to Adam. Paul understood Adam's trespass brought death and condemnation to humanity. By his disobedience, the many were made sinners and the trespass multiplied as the people struggled to live rightly under the Law.

Paul understood that the "free gift," mentioned five times in the above verses, is the grace of God and the act of Jesus's righteousness, his obedience to God, enables the many to be made righteous. Paul explains that through Jesus Christ our Lord, "where sin increased, grace abounded all the more." This abundance of grace comes through the one man, Jesus, bringing justification, righteousness, and eternal life for all.

Paul continues this line of thought in Romans 6:

> [10]*The death he died, he died to sin, once for all; but the life he lives, he lives to God.* [11]*So you also must consider yourselves dead to sin and alive to God in Christ Jesus.*

Beloved, Jesus manifested the bigness of God. He intentionally went to the people on the margins, people pushed aside, people undervalued. He didn't wait for humanity to get things right but took action for the well-being of all creation. His life, death, and resurrection expanded God's love to all of humanity.

The resurrection continues to change everything! In this new reality, Jesus stands with us as the only faithful one, the only one who lived in a faithful relationship with God. And because of the faithfulness of Jesus, our relationship with God doesn't depend on us saying we're sorry. It doesn't rely on us turning away from something we've done or who we are. It isn't contingent on us making confession, asking for forgiveness, professing our faithfulness, or promising to do something in exchange for God's love.

This means that affiliating with a particular Christian denomination, belonging to a church, being baptized, reading the Bible, praying, going to confession, taking communion, and attending worship are not required, nor are they necessary, for God to love you. God loves you already!

The opportunity to belong to a church, be baptized, read the Bible, pray, make a confession, take communion, and attend worship are gifts from God. They are gifts that enable us to encounter the Holy in the midst of the ordinary. They draw us into a deeper understanding of who God is and who you are and bring us into a community with others. As gifts, they are tools for the spiritual journey, not items on a checklist that needs to be completed for God to love you.

When we make repentance, forgiveness, baptism, and church membership, something that people have to do before God loves them, they become obstacles to knowing God's love. By untying the knots and reframing these theological understandings, our spiritual life can be one of hope and compassion.

Questions to ponder

- How do you understand the word grace as it relates to God's love?

- What is your reaction to the statement that "the resurrection of Jesus changes everything"?

- What is your reaction to the notion that Jesus is faith and that he is the only faithful one?

- What questions, concerns, or insights do you have about this chapter?

SUMMARY OF PART 1:

Untangling the Knots

Untangling the knot of Biblical interpretation enables us to understand the fullness of God's love story, revealing the extent that God goes to pursue us. We see that God continuously extends love, forgiveness, and reconciliation over and over and over again. When we approach the Bible as the inspired Word of God, we make space for the nuances of the distinct books in the collection; we call the Bible. In addition to being a love story, the Bible is our book of faith. It is intended to deepen our understanding of who God is and who we are in a relationship with God, ourselves, and each other.

Untangling the knot that makes God's love dependent on what we do and say helps us realize that God already loves us. God loves us because of who God is, not because of anything we say or do. When we use hurtful tactics and manipulative messages to compel people to accept Jesus, we push people away from God. The truth is that God doesn't need us to say or do anything before God loves us; God loves us already.

Untangling the knot of a narrow view of God enables us to experience the fullness of God and the expansive ways that God interacts with humanity and the created world. When we expand our view of God, we can build relationships with people who follow a different religious path or claim no religious affiliation at all. This new perspective opens up possibilities and opportunities for us to learn from each other and celebrate the unique ways that the Divine is made known.

Untangling the knot that over-emphasizes brokenness shifts us away from the doctrine of Original Sin to a perspective that emphasizes Original Blessing. From the very beginning, God called the new creation "good" and humanity "very good." Over-emphasizing brokenness led to identifying humanity as inherently sinful. Untangling this knot encourages us to recognize that humans are not perfect creations. We exercise our will, make decisions, and take actions in ways that sometimes harm ourselves, others, and the world around us. Don't worry; we're not doomed. God's blessings flow through the ups and downs of life, as we live as imperfect people entirely accepted and loved.

Untangling the knot of theological understandings that create obstacles to God's love starts with acknowledging that the resurrection of Jesus changes everything. When God raised Jesus from the dead, a new reality came into the world. Now, humanity's relationship with God is based on the faithfulness of Jesus and not on our faith. God is not waiting for us to make a profession of faith, change our ways, ask for forgiveness, or be baptized before loving us. Because of the resurrection of Jesus, repentance, and forgiveness of sins are already a reality because they are God's gifts to us.

Now that the five common knots are untangled, the threads can be used to create a quilt of God's love.

PART 2

Revealing the Certainty of God's Love

*God our Lord would have us look to the Giver
and love Him more than His gift, keeping Him always
before our eyes, in our hearts, and in our thoughts.*

Saint Ignatius

CHAPTER 6

Wrapped in a Quilt of Love

Maybe you've noticed that blankets and quilts are important to us. Newborns are swaddled in blankets to comfort them. Babies and toddlers, perhaps older kids and adults too, tend to have a favorite blankey that they drag around. We give blankets and quilts to mark significant events in someone's life. People who are sick or recovering from an illness receive blankets for comfort and a reminder of love. Blankets are draped over couches and chairs to provide warmth as we rest from a busy day.

My mother made me a beautiful, soft quilt before I went away to college. She used different pieces of colorful fabric to make each side a unique pattern and color. In one corner of the quilt, she stitched my name, the date of my high school graduation, and her initials. Not only did it accompany me to college, but it also comforted me after my dad died and kept me warm in the middle of the night as I fed my daughters. I took it with me when I went to seminary, and when I was up late at night, it draped around my lap. While I've treasured this quilt for many years, it has become more important to me since my mother died. Currently, the quilt is on my bed. It adds an extra layer of warmth at night. Each night, I'm reminded of my mother's love as I drift off to sleep underneath the quilt.

After I got into bed the other night, I realized that I couldn't find my quilt. Usually, I pull the quilt up near my pillow before I get into bed, but that night I forgot. Laying in bed, I reached down to pull the quilt up, but I couldn't find it. Because the lights were already off in my bedroom, I couldn't see it either.

I jumped out of bed and turned on my bedside lamp. The quilt was no were to be seen. I tore through the other covers on the bed, searching for it. My husband came into the room to see what was happening and joined in to help. He got down on the floor to look under the bed. That's when he saw it. Surprisingly, the quilt had fallen between the mattress and the footboard of the bed. He reached to get it and then handed it to me. Tears of relief flooded my eyes as I held that quilt. I climbed back into bed and pulled the quilt up close to me.

My mother's love permeates every bit of this quilt. With the quilt wrapped around me, I feel comfortable, safe, and warm. As I rest beneath the quilt, my mom seems closer to me, and as I hold the quilt, all the ways she showed her love to me flood my heart and mind. While I don't bring my mother's quilt with me as I go about my day, I always know that it's there, waiting for me to return home. The quilt is a tangible sign of her love for me.

Beloved, God's love is like this quilt. It surrounds you completely. Unlike my mother's quilt that doesn't leave the house, God's love is always with you. Wrapped in the warmth and comfort of the quilt, of God's love, you always know that you are accepted, and loved.

Since the knots have all been untangled, God's abundant love for you is revealed. No longer is God's love constrained or hidden among the knots.

In part two, the quilt of God's love is assembled from the untangled threads revealing that God's love is:

- already given to you

- extravagant, encompassing, and empowering

- based on acceptance, not rejection; compassion, not cold-heartedness; inclusion, not exclusion; and peace, not despair

- filled with the blessings of joy, comfort, strength, hope, interconnectedness, and courage

- experienced by living with intention, humility, and balance and embracing paradox, mystery, yourself and others, and spiritual practices that nourish you.

CHAPTER 7

God's Love is a Gift

---

*There's no place where you might be now, or where you might
have been in the past, or where you might go in the future that
will ever be beyond the reach of God's grace—nowhere.*[8]

Tullian Tchividjian

J esus liked to use parables, short, simple stories that taught a
moral or spiritual lesson. Jesus used these teaching aids to
convey a profound spiritual truth in a way that was relatable
and understandable for the listener. So, to help illustrate how
the gift of God's love and blessing is yours, I share the
following parable.

---

[8] Tullian Tchividjian, *Surprised by Grace: God's Relentless Pursuit of Rebels*, (Wheaten,
IL: Crossway), 149.

The parable of the unopened gift

One beautiful day, two friends, Riley and Taylor, met for lunch at a favorite restaurant. They hadn't seen each other for a long time so they were quickly engrossed in conversation. They talked about everything: their families and jobs, their successes and struggles, their memories of days gone by, and their hopes for the future.

Near the end of lunch, Taylor surprised Riley with a gift. This flustered Riley since they weren't accustomed to giving gifts to each other. Without opening the gift, Riley expressed thanksgiving for their friendship and time together. Promising to open the gift later, Riley quickly placed it in a bag. They said their good-byes, promised to get together again soon, and then went their separate ways. When Riley got home, the still-wrapped gift was placed on a desk.

For a while, the gift was visible every time Riley walked past the desk. Riley would often look at the gift and think, *I really should open this sometime, but not today because I'm too busy.* Over time, the unopened gift gathered dust. One day, Riley picked up the gift again, blew off the dust, and thought I should open this today. But then Riley remembered that there was something else to do so the gift was placed back on the desk. Once again, the gift collected dust and other things covered it up.

After some time, Taylor and Riley saw each other at a social event. After saying "hello," Taylor asked if Riley was enjoying the gift. Embarrassed, Riley confessed that the gift remained unopened, that, unfortunately, it was out of sight and out of mind. Seeing Taylor's disappointment, Riley promised to open the gift right away.

Returning home, Riley went directly to the desk which was piled high with books, chargers, papers, and other random things. There were so many things piled on top of each other that it took some time to remove the different layers. Then to Riley's surprise and disappointment, the gift was nowhere to be found. Riley looked under the desk, in the closet, and then just before giving up, the wrapped gift was spotted on top of the bookcase that was next to the desk. Apparently, at some point, Riley must have moved the gift and then completely forgotten about it.

Blowing off the dust, Riley admired the neatly wrapped package and opened it. As the lid was lifted off, a warm scarf in the colors of their college alma mater appeared. Riley lifted the scarf out of the box and, upon seeing its beauty, was filled with thanksgiving, regret, and sadness. You see, the gift was received in early fall and remained unopened through the cold season of winter. Riley missed the opportunity to wear the scarf on those bitterly cold days, missed the opportunity to wear the scarf to college gatherings, and missed the opportunity to let the scarf provide comfort and protection throughout the season.

The truth is that the gift always belonged to Riley. It wasn't taken away because it remained unopened. It didn't diminish over time. Instead, the gift remained intact just as it had been given to Riley. And the scarf, something intended to make a difference in Riley's life, was left inside the box.

Beloved, you too have received a gift. This gift comes to you from God. Paul writes in Ephesians 2:

> [4]*But God, who is rich in mercy, out of the great love with which he loved us* [5]*even when we were dead through our trespasses, made us alive together with Christ—by grace you have been saved—* [6]*and raised us up with him and seated us with him in the heavenly places in Christ Jesus,* [7]*so that in the ages to come he might show the immeasurable riches of his grace in kindness toward us in Christ Jesus.* [8]*For by grace you have been saved through faith, and this is not your own doing; it is the gift of God—* [9]*not the result of works, so that no one may boast.*

Because God is the initiator and giver of this gift, no one can take it away from you, nor can you lose it. This gift is completely and eternally yours. No matter what happens in your life, where your life choices take you, this gift remains yours, not because of who you are but because of who the giver is.

The gift that God gives to you is wrapped in unconditional and unconstrained love. Another name for this love is grace.

It is loaded with blessings that God expects will inspire, comfort, and strengthen you. It is intended to enfold you in joy, hope, courage, and interconnectedness. Beloved, God gives this gift to you so that you know you are always and forever loved by the one who created you. God longs for this gift to carry you through the ups and downs and the back and forth of life.

What you do with this gift is up to you. You can, like Riley, put it on top of a bookcase and forget about it. You can ignore it for so long that it gets covered in dust. You can admire it from afar and promise one day to open it. You can throw it away unopened, never knowing its contents. Or, you can open the gift and let it make a difference in your life.

Beloved, your acceptance by God is not dependent on you opening this gift. God already accepts you completely. The gift is already yours; the blessings contained within the gift are already yours. When you open the gift, you reveal the blessings which enable you to live fully in the here and now.

Questions to ponder

- Have you ever received a gift and then failed to open it until prompted by the gift-giver? What did that feel like?

- How does the notion of God as the giver, initiator, of the gift fit with your understanding of how God interacts in your life?

- What is your reaction to the notion that God has given you a gift which can never be lost or taken away?

- How does that fit with your understanding of God's love?

- What questions, thoughts, and concerns do you have about this chapter?

CHAPTER 8

Revealing the
Nature of God's Love

Christ expressed all his teachings in his last commandment:
"love each other, as I have loved you." Everyone will see that
you are my disciples, if you love each other. He did not say,
"if you believe," but "if you love." Faith can change over time,
because our knowledge is constantly changing. Love, on
the contrary, never changes; love is eternal.

Leo Tolstoy

One of my favorite authors, Henri Nouwen, had the opportunity to travel with the Flying Rodleighs, a troupe of trapeze artists who performed with the German circus Simoneit-Barum. Inevitably, their conversations turned to flying and how they could do what they did. Nouwen said, in the end, it comes down to this: "A flyer must fly, and a catcher must catch, and the flyer must trust, with outstretched arms, that his catcher will be there for him."[9]

As a Dutch Catholic priest, Nouwen understood this as a metaphor for what happens to us when we die. He writes, "Dying is trusting in the catcher. To care for the dying is to say, 'Don't be afraid. Remember that you are a beloved child of God. He will be there when you make your long jump. Don't try to grab him, he will grab you. Just stretch out your arms and hands and trust, trust, trust.'"[10]

This metaphor is indeed a beautiful way to think about the movement from life through death and into eternal life. It also works well as a metaphor for God's loving relationship with us in life.

Beloved, God created us to fly, to soar through our lives, becoming all that God has created us to be. As we fly, we will experience the ups and downs of the natural rhythm that is life. Sometimes the back and forth of flight will be smooth; other times, it will challenge us in many ways. Sometimes we'll fly alone, and other times other trapeze flyers will soar beside us as companions in flight. Throughout life, we will

---

[9] Henri Nouwen, *Our Greatest Gift: A Meditation on Dying and Caring,* (New York: HarperCollins, 1995), 67.

[10] Ibid.

transfer from one trapeze to another as we grow, learn, and embrace more fully our unique gifts, passions, and skills.

Along the way, we may need to jump into the waiting arms of another flyer, who is functioning as a catcher for us. This transfer requires an enormous level of trust from the one who is flying and cooperation from the catcher. As we make these transfers, we discover that God guides the catcher we need in a particular situation to be there for us and empowers them with the strength to catch us. The give and take of this relationship will shape our lives as we support, mentor, and encourage one another along the way. Each of us, at some time or another, will be flyers and catchers.

The ultimate catcher as we soar through our lives is God. When we let go of the trapeze bar to fly into unknown situations or to explore new opportunities, God is ready to catch us. Reaching out to grasp the next bar takes a lot of courage. Hopefully, we'll take hold of it with a firm grip, but that's not always possible. Sometimes we'll miss the bar, and in those instances, we can trust that God, our catcher, will grab hold of us.

At times we may want to swing back and forth on the same trapeze bar for a while to breathe or to enjoy what is happening around us. When we need to rest and get off the trapeze for a while, we can fall into the waiting net below us. This net is God's profound love for us, a love that is always there for you because that is the nature of God's gift of love.

The three-fold nature of God's love

It's extravagant

It catches you from wherever and whenever you fall. No matter how many times you fall into the net, it will catch you. Whether you fall into the net intentionally, accidentally, or by some other circumstance, it doesn't matter. The net of God's love has no limitations. It doesn't run out or fail with overuse or underuse. It doesn't function like a lottery ticket, where you need to select the right numbers in order to receive some reward. The extravagant net of God's love is not contingent on you having the right beliefs, or right thoughts, or right actions. It's not contingent on how often you go to church, read your Bible, or pray. It's not contingent on your membership in a congregation. It's not contingent on how often you take communion or if you're baptized. And it's not contingent on the quality or quantity of your life. The extravagant net of God's love will catch you because that's who God is.

> ⁹*God's love was revealed among us in this way: God sent his only Son into the world so that we might live through him.* ¹⁰*In this is love, not that we loved God but that he loved us and sent his Son to be the atoning sacrifice for our sins.* ¹¹*Beloved, since God loved us so much, we also ought to love one another.* ¹²*No one has ever seen God; if we love one another, God lives in us, and his love is perfected in us (1 John 4).*

It's encompassing

It embraces every aspect of who you are: the good, the bad, the ugly, and the beautiful. God's steadfast love and mercy encompass you. The net of God's love is not temporary or transactional. It will not be taken away from you for any reason. You don't need to change your behavior before God loves you. You don't need to exchange something that you have, like your good intentions or your apologies, to receive the love that God has for you. You don't need to accept Jesus before he loves you. The encompassing net of God's love embraces you because of who God is, not because of who you are. God doesn't wait for you to get life right or to love God rightly; instead, God loves you first.

[8]I [Paul] pray that you may have the power to comprehend, with all the saints, what is the breadth and length and height and depth, [19]and to know the love of Christ that surpasses knowledge, so that you may be filled with all the fullness of God (Ephesians 3).

It's empowering

Being the recipient of God's extravagant and encompassing love empowers you to live fully. You're set free from everything that constrains you and can live in the freedom that God always intended for you. Through this empowering net of God's love, you can try new things, go on new adventures, learn new skills, and develop new passions. Because of the empowering net of God's love, you can love others, care for your neighbor, make mistakes, take risks, and wander down uncertain paths. You are set free for all of this because of God's love for you.

> [16]Now may our Lord Jesus Christ himself and God our Father, who loved us and through grace gave us eternal comfort and good hope, [17]comfort your hearts and strengthen them in every good work and word (2 Thessalonians 2).

What this means for us

Because of the extravagant, encompassing, and empowering love of God, you may fly from a trapeze bar to a trapeze bar, knowing that you are okay, that all is well with you.

Now don't get me wrong. This doesn't mean that life will be easy for you. You will still face challenges, hardships, problems, disappointments, and roadblocks along the way. But you will experience none of this alone.

God will be with you. God's extravagant net of love will never fail you. It will expand beyond your wildest imagination to cover every aspect of what life has in store for you.

The encompassing net of God's love will cover you with comfort when you feel pain, hope when you face despair, joy when sorrows abound, and peace when the troubles of this world threaten to overwhelm you.

And the empowering net of God's love will enable you to keep on living, to keep on trying, to keep on being the you God created you to be.

As you fly through life, moving from a trapeze bar to a trapeze bar, God's love will carry you along. And one day, when it's your time to reach for the Great Catcher, the Holy One, you will stretch out your arms, and the one who has loved you from the beginning will catch you with open arms.

Questions to ponder

- How does the image of a trapeze artist flying from bar to bar as a metaphor for life resonate with you?

- What is your experience of being the flyer and the catcher as you fly with others?

- When have you fallen into the net of God's love? What was that like for you?

- How has the three-fold nature of God's love: extravagant, encompassing, and empowering impacted your life?

- What questions, thoughts, and concerns do you have about this chapter?

CHAPTER 9

Revealing the Attributes of God's Love

Unending Love

I am loved by an unending love.
I am embraced by arms that find me
even when I am hidden from myself.
I am touched by fingers that soothe me
even when I am too proud for soothing.
I am counseled by voices that guide me
even when I am too embittered to hear.
I am loved by an unending love.

I am supported by hands that uplift me
even in the midst of a fall.
I am urged on by eyes that meet me
even when I am too weak for meeting.
I am loved by an unending love.

Embraces, touched, soothed, and counseled;
may mine too be arms and fingers,
the voice and the hands,
the eyes and the smile
that compels another to say:
"I am loved by an unending love."[11]

Rami Shapiro

Beloved, you are loved by an unending love. Acceptance, compassion, inclusion, and peace and the attributes of God's extravagant, encompassing, empowering and unending love.

Acceptance, not rejection

Because God loves us completely and shows this love by choosing us, we have acceptance from God, not rejection. So many times, throughout the written story of God's interaction with humanity, God could have rejected humanity, could have turned away from all that was created. Thankfully, that didn't happen. Instead, God continued to pursue humanity

---

[11] Rami M. Shapiro, *Accidental Grace: Poetry, Prayers, and Psalms*, (Brewster, MA: Paraclete Press, 2015), 38-39.

and to give second, third, and fourth chances until ultimately God did a new thing in Jesus. This passage from Paul's letter to the people of Rome explains it:

> *⁶For while we were still weak, at the right time Christ died for the ungodly. ⁷Indeed, rarely will anyone die for a righteous person— though perhaps for a good person someone might actually dare to die. ⁸But God proves his love for us in that while we still were sinners Christ died for us. ⁹Much more surely then, now that we have been justified by his blood, will we be saved through him from the wrath of God. ¹⁰For if while we were enemies, we were reconciled to God through the death of his Son, much more surely, having been reconciled, will we be saved by his life (Romans 5).*

God loves the "skunky" people

While I was a seminary student, I attended a meeting for Lutheran pastors, staff, and lay leaders. At the time, the Evangelical Lutheran Church in America (ELCA) was debating if and how to include gay and lesbian people in committed relationships as pastors and leaders in the church. This was an agonizing debate for me personally because my daughter is a lesbian who has experienced the pain of not being accepted by the church. She often told me that she was tired of being "the problem that church people keep talking about." For me, this was not a debate about those people over there, people unknown to me. Instead, it was a debate about the inclusion of my daughter and others like her in the church where I was preparing to serve as an ordained pastor.

When our daughter first came out, we needed to reconcile all that we had believed previously about homosexuality and God's acceptance. Over time, I recognized that what I wanted for my daughter was for her to be loved, supported, and able to be her best self in the world. It didn't matter what her sexuality was. She's my daughter, and I love her completely just as she is.

Back at this meeting, I was sitting in the meeting hall listening to passionate debates on both sides. Tempers were raging and some were using hurtful language. I became so upset that I left the auditorium to get some fresh air. The meeting was held on a college campus, so I started walking around the grounds, pacing back and forth on the sidewalks. Ultimately, I ended up walking a circular path in the courtyard of some dormitories.

As I walked, a skunk ran across the sidewalk in front of me to the inside of the courtyard. I stopped and looked at this creature, unsure what to do next. She stopped and looked at me, probably trying to figure out what to do with me. Then she scratched at the dirt and started walking near the sidewalk. She looked back at me several times as if beckoning me to walk with her. And so, I did.

We walked along together for several loops around the courtyard. Every now and then, the skunk would stop, scratch the dirt, look at me, and then resume walking. Each time the skunk stopped, I stopped. And every time she started again; I resumed my walking. The skunk and I became so comfortable with each other that I started talking to her, wondering out loud, what in the world are we doing, what is the church doing, and where is God in everything that is happening?

With every pass around the courtyard, I expected the skunk to run back across the sidewalk into the woods. It took several loops before that happened. But, before the skunk ran back across my path and into the woods, she scratched the dirt from inside the loop and then again on the outside of the loop, each time looking up at me. I admit that I was awestruck about my encounter with this beautiful, and often feared, creature. Alone now, I walked around the courtyard again before heading to my room.

Thankfully, my roommate was already in the room. She expressed concern for me and wondered what I'd been doing. I explained my experience with the skunk and revealed my troubled feelings about the church's behavior. I told her that I was questioning whether I should continue preparing to be a pastor. I wondered how I could serve as a pastor in a denomination that failed to embrace my daughter, whom I loved, and people like her.

My dear roommate, friend, and mentor suggested that maybe the visit from the skunk was God's way of reminding me that we are all "skunky" people, people who can be smelly and cause others to be afraid; and people who can also be beautiful and show us a different way. She suggested that maybe God was calling me to walk with the "skunky" people and to love and accept them as God loves and accepts me.

In the coming days, weeks, and months, I reflected on this. I did continue in my preparation to become an ordained pastor in the ELCA and was ordained in 2006. In 2009, the ELCA voted to allow gay and lesbian people in committed relationships to serve as pastors and rostered leaders in the church. Not all congregations and members of the ELCA agreed with this decision so it caused sadness and uncertainty as people and congregations voted to leave the ELCA. Other members and congregations celebrated this decision even as we mourned for the division that occurred. Now, more than 10 years later, the ELCA, and most of its congregations, are embracing an explicit welcome to people of all sexualities and gender identities.

Beloved, you are a beautiful creation of God, unlike anyone else, and God has gifted you with personality, passions, interests, skills, talents, and experiences. Each of these makes you uniquely you! There is no one else like you.

You may have heard that you are somehow unworthy of God's love because of some dimension of who you are. You may have heard that you need to change so that God will love and accept you. None of this is true. It's time to let go of these harmful and hurtful messages and embrace yourself as the beloved child of God you truly are.

God created you just as you are, and loves you completely. Every aspect of who you are reveals how God intends for you to be in this world. This passage from Ephesians highlights the expansive and unconditional nature of God's acceptance:

> *⁴But God, who is rich in mercy, out of the great love with which he loved us ⁵even when we were dead through our trespasses, made us alive together with Christ—by grace you have been saved— ⁶and raised us up with him and seated us with him in the heavenly places in Christ Jesus, ⁷so that in the ages to come he might show the immeasurable riches of his grace in kindness toward us in Christ Jesus (Ephesians 2).*

Beloved, God didn't wait for us to become less skunky. Didn't wait for us to achieve some kind of ideal. God didn't wait for humanity to get things right. Didn't wait for us to accept Jesus as our Lord and Savior. Didn't wait for us to ask for forgiveness or make a profession of faith. Instead, God took action, takes action, first. God's acceptance of you, me, all people, and all creation, is at God's initiative!

Compassion, not cold-heartedness

Compassion and loving-kindness are the very essence of God's heart. There are so many passages of scripture that proclaim God's compassion for humanity and all creation. One of my favorites is in Isaiah 43:

>*¹But now thus says the LORD, he who created you, O Jacob, he who formed you, O Israel: Do not fear, for I have redeemed you; I have called you by name, you are mine. ²When you pass through the waters, I will be with you; and through the rivers, they shall not overwhelm you; when you walk through fire you shall not be burned, and the flame shall not consume you. ³For I am the LORD your God, the Holy One of Israel, your Savior. I give Egypt as your ransom, Ethiopia and Seba in exchange for you.⁴Because you are precious in my sight, and honored, and I love you.*

These words of the Lord from Isaiah reveal God's compassion. Beloved, hear the Lord say to you: I have redeemed you. I have called you by name. You are mine. I will be with you. I am the Lord, your God, the Holy One of Israel, your Savior. You are precious in my sight and honored. I love you. Let these words sink in your heart, fill your thoughts, and nourish your spirit.

God never leaves you

While I have experienced God's compassion many times, I remember one time in particular. My dad died in 1983 at the age of 42 from complications related to a massive heart attack. My mom was 41, I was just 24 years old, and my sister was 17. My husband and I were expecting our second child. Needless to say, Daddy was too young to die, and we were too young to lose a husband and a father. My sadness and anger at Daddy's death turned toward God. I just couldn't make sense of why my dad's life would be cut short. He was preparing to retire from the US Army so they could move to Raleigh to be near us and our growing family. My anger caused me to put walls between myself and God. While I knew this was irrational anger, as God didn't cause Daddy to die, I simply wanted nothing to do with the God who didn't save my dad from death.

For 10 years, I turned away from God. I built walls around myself, separating myself from God. I stopped attending worship, stopped praying, stopped doing anything related to spirituality. I was clearly in the wilderness. Yet, God never turned away from me. God never stopped loving me. Instead, God came to me through the caring actions of others who held me close when my sorrow overwhelmed me, who prayed for me when I couldn't pray myself, and who extended compassion and kindness to me.

My mom coped with Daddy's death differently than I did. When she was able, she returned to worship and eventually started taking our daughters with her. Over time, they begged us to attend so we could hear them sing in the children's choir or see them participate in some way. I attended reluctantly and didn't feel comfortable in that space. About 10 years later, yes, it took that long, I agreed to attend a spiritual retreat sponsored by our congregation. At the retreat, I took the opportunity to talk with one of the pastors about my pain and anger. The pastor gave me the greatest gift when he told me that "God can handle your anger."

Well, of course, God can handle my anger! This is such a simple truth but hearing it from this pastor set me free to grieve. You see, I was embarrassed that I was still grieving and that I harbored anger toward God. This sense of embarrassment held me hostage to my grief and anger. Now that I'd been told that it was okay to be angry at God, I felt like I could grieve in a much healthier way. This began my road toward healing. My grief never went away, but eventually, I learned how to live more fully with that grief. As I let my guard down and allowed myself to be loved and blessed by God, I experienced the deep compassion of the Lord who says, "You are precious in my sight, and I love you."

I realized that by pushing God away, I missed out on the comfort and peace that God intended for me. Thank goodness, God didn't wait for me to come to my senses;

instead, God pursued me and continued to extend compassion and loving-kindness to me.

God gives us the gift of repentance out of compassion

God's compassion is always present. It is not contingent on anything. Despite my anger toward God, loving-kindness was always mine. So often we believe that to receive God's mercy, we have to ask for forgiveness. Thinking this way makes God's compassion contingent on our actions, our choices, our apologies, and our promises to change our ways. Beloved, this way of thinking isn't helpful and doesn't reflect God's way of loving you. The truth is that God's compassion and loving-kindness are gifts freely given to you by God.

God doesn't need our apologies or promises to change our ways in order to love us. God isn't waiting for us to request forgiveness before God forgives us. Forgiveness and love are gifts for our benefit. Bring to mind a time when you did something wrong, something that harmed you or someone you love. How did that feel? How did that impact your relationship with the other person?

When I do something that hurts someone, I might avoid the person or live in regret and embarrassment, hoping that it will all go away. This behavior isn't helpful and only makes life uncomfortable for both of us. A healthier response is to admit what I've done, apologize, and seek reconciliation.

Our relationship with God is much the same as our relationship with others. There are times when we might believe that we've done or said something which disappoints or angers God. When this happens, we might choose to avoid God by ceasing to pray or coming to worship. We might tell ourselves that we've lost God's love completely. None of this is helpful. Remember, God's love is not dependent or contingent on you!

To help ease our burdens and anxieties, God gives us the gifts of repentance and forgiveness. They are not things we do to earn God's love. Instead, they are gifts meant to set us free from the embarrassment, pain, and regret we carry and restore our relationships.

We need to extend that compassion to others

Being able to forgive someone who has harmed us is also a gift. Harboring a lack of forgiveness toward someone is like holding a hot coal in your hands. The person that you haven't forgiven has probably moved on and no longer remembers what happened to fracture your relationship. Yet you are still holding that hot piece of coal. It's hurting you. It's paralyzing you. It's keeping you from moving forward.

God gives you the ability to forgive so you can let go of the hurts and pains inflicted upon you and release the hot coal. Forgiveness doesn't mean that you need to forget about what happened; some things in life need to be remembered, so they don't hurt you again. Forgiveness doesn't mean that you need to go back to the way things were before the person hurt you; some relationships in life can't be restored. Forgiving the hurt done to you is for your benefit. It sets you free and enables you to live a more abundant life. Sure, the other person may benefit from your ability to forgive the hurt that was done to you, which is a gift that you can extend to that person.

Beloved, there is no condemnation, no punishment in the words of the Lord through the prophet Isaiah, quoted earlier in this chapter. God's compassion embraces you completely, not because of anything you've done or said. God has compassion for you because of who God is and because of who you are, God's beloved creation.

Inclusion, not exclusion

My oldest daughter and her wife adopted three children through the foster care system in our county. Having given birth to both of my daughters and not having much interaction with adoptive parents or their children, I was woefully unaware of the unique relationship established through adoption. It wasn't until my daughter and her wife decided to pursue adoption as a means of bringing children into their family that I began to understand the truth of what adoption does for the one being adopted and for the family whose love compels them to choose adoption.

One day, my daughter and her wife received information about a ten-year-old boy and a seven-year-old girl, a brother and sister, who were available for adoption. Although they weren't sure about adopting siblings, they decided to meet the children. After several months of getting to know each other, the children and my daughter and her wife decided to move forward in the adoption process together. The children moved into their home and a new family was created. Not long after the children were adopted, their baby sister was born to their birth mother. The social worker called and asked if this new family of four could become a family of five. They all said yes and so three days after her birth, the baby came to live with her forever family.

The process of fostering and adopting these children brought clarity to the use of the word adoption in Paul's letter to the Ephesians. Simply put, being adopted means being chosen.

> *[3]Blessed be the God and Father of our Lord Jesus Christ, who has blessed us in Christ with every spiritual blessing in the heavenly places, [4]just as he chose us in Christ before the foundation of the world to be holy and blameless before him in love. [5]He destined us for adoption as his children through Jesus Christ, according to the good pleasure of his will, [6]to the praise of his glorious grace that he freely bestowed on us in the Beloved. [7]In him we have redemption*

through his blood, the forgiveness of our trespasses, according to the riches of his grace [8]that he lavished on us" (Ephesians 1).

So often we think that we have to do something or say something to be included in God's love. The truth is that God chose us from the beginning as it says, God "chose us in Christ before the foundation of the world." God created us for relationship, companionship, and when that went sideways, God continued to embrace humanity. Over and over again, God chose humanity. When it became clear that humankind couldn't maintain a relationship with God, God took action in Jesus. Jesus is the Beloved that Paul mentions. It is because of Jesus, because of the Beloved, that we have redemption and forgiveness.

The words that Paul uses to describe the extent that God goes to include us make the point that our inclusion is all about what God does: [God's] good pleasure, [God's] glorious grace, [God] freely bestowed on us, riches of [God's] grace, [God] lavished on us. We are included because God chooses us!

Peace, not despair

Just as God reached out to humanity with compassion, inclusion, and acceptance, God also established peace with creation.

22The LORD spoke to Moses, saying: 23Speak to Aaron and his sons, saying, Thus you shall bless the Israelites: You shall say to them, 24The LORD bless you and keep you; 25the LORD make his face to shine upon you, and be gracious to you; 26the LORD lift up his countenance upon you, and give you peace (Numbers 6).

This Psalm speaks of the gift of God's peace:

10For the mountains may depart, and the hills be removed, but my steadfast love shall not depart from you, and my covenant of peace shall not be removed, says the LORD, who has compassion on you (Psalm 54).

Despite the many ways that the Israelites failed to live faithfully, the Lord extended blessing, grace, and peace to them. We, too, have received blessing, grace, and peace from God. The Lord indicates that while everything else may come tumbling down, steadfast love will not depart, and the covenant of peace will never fail. All of this is because of God's compassion.

These words of Jesus continue this message of peace:

27Peace I leave with you; my peace I give to you. I do not give to you as the world gives. Do not let your hearts be troubled, and do not let them be afraid (John 14).

God's action in Jesus restores everything that was torn apart and diminished in the earlier interactions with God. Paul explains our peace with God in this way:

> *¹Therefore, since we are justified by faith, we have peace with God through our Lord Jesus Christ, ²through whom we have obtained access to this grace in which we stand; and we boast in our hope of sharing the glory of God (Romans 5).*

What God's peace means for us

God's peace doesn't mean an absence of pain or suffering; it doesn't guarantee that our lives will be easy or that everything will go our way. Instead, God's peace is about God's commitment to remain in a relationship with us. Because of God's peace, we need not fear what happens to us when we die. Because of God's peace, we know that God will never turn away from us, never abandon us. Because of God's peace, nothing separates us from the love of God.

> *³¹What then are we to say about these things? If God is for us, who is against us? ³²He who did not withhold his own Son, but gave him up for all of us, will he not with him also give us everything else? ³³Who will bring any charge against God's elect? It is God who justifies. ³⁴Who is to condemn? It is Christ Jesus, who died, yes, who was raised, who is at the right hand of God, who indeed*

intercedes for us. [35] Who will separate us from the love of Christ? Will hardship, or distress, or persecution, or famine, or nakedness, or peril, or sword? [37] No, in all these things we are more than conquerors through him who loved us. [38] For I [Paul] am convinced that neither death, nor life, nor angels, nor rulers, nor things present, nor things to come, nor powers, [39] nor height, nor depth, nor anything else in all creation, will be able to separate us from the love of God in Christ Jesus our Lord (Romans 8).

My mother was diagnosed with stage four lung cancer in 2008. After undergoing a round of treatment, she elected to stop pursuing lifesaving, curative measures and enrolled in hospice care. My husband, sister, and I along with the help of many others provided round-the-clock care and support to mom. As time went by and she got sicker and sicker, our conversations often turned to the nature of death and peace with God.

My mother was active in her congregation, participated in Bible study, and lived her faith in her interactions with others. Her faith provided comfort for her when her husband, my dad, died in 1983. Her faith enabled her to rebuild her life as she embraced who she was as a widow for 25 years. Now facing her death, she began to voice her anxieties and fears.

One day, Mom and I were enjoying some quiet conversation.

She said to me, "Tell me it's not all a lie."

"What do you mean Mom, what's not a lie?" I asked.

Mom clarified, "That God really does love me unconditionally, that when I die, I'll be with Jesus. Tell me that's not a lie."

My heart broke for her. Here is this beloved child of God who trusted in God for everything, now giving voice to her doubts. I know that she'd heard the promises of God many times in her life, but now, when it mattered most, the promises didn't seem to comfort her.

I pulled out my Bible and turned to one of my favorite passages from Romans, chapter 8. I read to her:

> [38]*For I am convinced that neither death, nor life, nor angels, nor rulers, nor things present, nor things to come, nor powers,* [39]*nor height, nor depth, nor anything else in all creation, will be able to separate us from the love of God in Christ Jesus our Lord.*

I reminded her that facing death himself, Job knew that he would see God (Job 19). I assured her that she, too, would see God when she gathered at the feast that has no end. We talked about the many rooms in God's house and that Jesus has prepared one for her (John 14). This made her chuckle as she wondered if she'd have a roommate. We concluded that Daddy was already waiting there for her.

These passages seemed to bring her some peace and she drifted off to sleep. But my spirit was troubled, my heart was broken, and I went outside to let off some steam. It was a beautiful November day. The sky was clear, and the wind was calm. I didn't want to wander too far from her house, so I paced in her driveway and out into the cul-de-sac. The more I paced, the more agitated I became. I raised my trembling hands to heaven and shouted, "You better not make a liar out of me!"

All of a sudden, boom! A large branch from a tree close to the driveway came crashing down at my feet. I stood there looking up at the tree and down at the branch lying at my feet.

"Okay, so this is how you prove your presence and answer prayer!" I said out loud.

I reached down, picked up that branch, and carried it with me as I paced some more. Each time I walked past that tree, I looked up at it, trying to see where the branch broke off. The tree looked pristine. There was no evidence of where that branch used to be. I realized there was no reason for this branch to have fallen at my feet. No reason at all, except by the grace of God.

I shook my head and looking up, I said, "Thanks for your love and presence in all this mess!"

I carried the branch into the house, and when Mom woke up, I told her what happened and showed her the branch.

Handing her the branch, I said, "Mom, I prayed for you to have peace, for God to show you in a tangible way that God is with you now, that you are loved, and that there is nothing to fear. God answered my prayer by throwing this branch at me." We sat quietly together as Mom cradled the branch.

We live in difficult times, and many things can rattle our peace. Our thoughts and doubts can make us uneasy about who we are and who God is. Situations affect us from outside of ourselves, which can cause us to question our worthiness, to wonder if God loves us. We've learned to be suspicious of things that sound too good to be true.

We've heard that giving voice to our doubts indicates a lack of faith and that this lack of faith negatively impacts our relationship with God. Beloved, that's not true at all. Doubt is a natural reality in how we approach life and faith. It's a reminder that we are not perfect creations. It's hard to accept that God is active in your life when everything around you is falling apart. You can do two things with your doubt: you can let it paralyze you or cause you to reject something altogether or you can use your doubt to propel you into a search for understanding.

Beloved, there is no need to deny your doubt about God and faith. Just as God can handle your anger, God can embrace your doubt. Philip Yancy says it this way, "One bold message in the Book of Job is that you can say anything to God. Throw at him your grief, your anger, your doubt, your bitterness, your betrayal, your disappointment—he can absorb them all."[12] See your doubt as a gift from God intended to draw you into exploration, discovery, and a deeper awareness of who God is.

Choose peace instead of fear and despair

Doubt and suspicion, anxiety and fear about God's relationship with us causes undue distress for people. It can have a negative influence on the decisions people make about their involvement with the church and their relationship with God. Two phrases frequently appear in scripture. In both the Old and New Testaments, the phrase "do not fear" appears 43 times and the phrase "do not be afraid" appears 59 times. It's clear that the Holy One does not want us to be fearful, to be afraid, because fear limits our capacity to love and be loved.

---

[12] Philip Yancy, *Disappointment with God: Three Questions No One Asks Aloud*, (Grand Rapids, MI: Zondervan, 2015), 263.

¹²As God's chosen ones, holy and beloved, clothe yourselves with compassion, kindness, humility, meekness, and patience. ¹³Bear with one another and, if anyone has a complaint against another, forgive each other; just as the Lord has forgiven you, so you also must forgive. ¹⁴Above all, clothe yourselves with love, which binds everything together in perfect harmony. ¹⁵And let the peace of Christ rule in your hearts, to which indeed you were called in the one body. And be thankful (Colossians 3).

Beloved, ruminate on these words. Let them sink into the deepest recesses of your heart, mind, and spirit. You are God's chosen one. You are holy and beloved. God covers you with compassion, kindness, humility, meekness, patience, and love. Experience the warmth of this embrace and let it calm your weariness, reduce your anxiety, and restore your peace.

Peace brings love

God not only wants you to experience peace; God wants you to be a person of peace. Clothing yourself with compassion, kindness, humility, meekness, patience, and love is about extending these virtues to yourself. In essence, it's about being gentle with yourself when things don't go as you'd hoped or when you make a mistake or do something that harmed yourself or someone else.

As you live in your beloved-ness, you have the opportunity to recognize others as God's chosen ones, also holy and beloved. And just as God is gentle with you and you are gentle with yourself, you can be gentle with others. In this way, we bear with each other in love, share each other's burdens, and support one another in this journey called life.

Colossians 3:14 continues with "above all, clothe yourselves with love, which binds everything together in perfect harmony."

Love is the glue that brings everything and everyone into harmony. Our love toward the Holy One, ourselves, and each other is always flawed because we are not perfect people. God's love, *agape* love, is the love that embraces us and binds us together, as individuals and as the human family. *Agape* love is unconditional, complete, certain, and perfect. It creates perfect harmony, perfect relationship.

Beloved, remember whose we are, "God's chosen ones," and who we are, "holy and beloved." Being clothed with compassion, kindness, humility, meekness, patience, and love while linking arms with each other and sharing each other's burdens is what makes for peace.

[15] And let the peace of Christ rule in your hearts, to which indeed you were called in the one body (Galatians 3).

Trust in peace

This peace is not our own. We do not generate it. Instead, we share in the peace of the Holy One. This peace is the only perfect peace, the only everlasting peace. This peace is what will carry us through the ups and downs of life. We can trust this peace and experience this peace when everything feels like it's falling apart, because this peace doesn't waver or depend on us in any way. It is a gift to us and for us.

Beloved, the Holy One does not want you to be afraid. You belong to God and because of God's love, all is well with your soul.

> [10]*Do not fear, for I am with you, do not be afraid, for I am your God; I will strengthen you, I will help you, I will uphold you with my victorious right hand (Isaiah 41).*
>
> [8]*The LORD is gracious and merciful, slow to anger and abounding in steadfast love.* [9]*The LORD is good to all, and his compassion is over all that he has made (Psalm 145).*

Summary

The attributes of God's love are exemplified by acceptance, not rejection; compassion, not cold-heartedness; inclusion, not exclusion; and peace, not despair. Regardless of what we do or don't do, say or don't say, it is God's initiative to accept, love, include, and make peace with us. That's what makes it a gift! When we think that we have to do something to earn God's love or need to behave a certain way to keep God's love, we diminish the quality of this love, and it is no longer the gift that God intends it to be.

8For by grace you have been saved through faith, and this is not your own doing; it is the gift of God— 9not the result of works, so that no one may boast (Ephesians 2).

We have received an amazing gift! It comes freely and without reservation or hesitation to humanity and all creation. With this gift we can live in the peace of God's love through the ups and downs of our life. Confident that we are accepted, loved, and included not because of who we are but because of who God is.

Questions to ponder

- Which attribute resonates with you and in what way?

- Which attribute challenges you and in what way?

- How do these four attributes of God's gift of love impact your life now?

- What questions, thoughts, and concerns do you have about this chapter?

CHAPTER 10

Revealing the Blessings of God's Love

Our greatest enemy is fear: compassion-crippling, hope-choking, courage-stifling, mission-killing fear. Our greatest ally is God's love: compassion-growing, hope-stoking, courage-lifting, mission-building love.

Unknown

Earlier I shared a parable with you about someone who received a gift and then set it aside for a time before opening it. The receiver missed opportunities to let the gift make a difference in their life. Now let me share a true story about giving gifts.

I once purchased a gift for a dear friend. I knew it was something she wanted because I was with her when she admired it. I wasn't going to see her for a while, so I kept the gift in the bag and put it in my closet for safekeeping. Months went by, and I forgot all about the present. The occasion came, and having forgotten about the earlier purchase; I picked up something else for her. She graciously received my gift, and life continued for both of us. It wasn't until I was preparing to move that I came across the bag in my closet. Confused, I opened it, and to my surprise, there was the vase that my friend had admired, and I had purchased, just for her.

Holding that vase brought tears to my eyes as I remembered how much she liked it. I called my friend right away and told her what I'd found. She was thrilled to hear that I'd purchased it for her and was grateful to receive it.

God is a gift-giver. The difference is that God doesn't stash the gift away for a day when the receiver might ask for it, really need it, or appreciate it. Instead, God gives the gift at the very beginning of the relationship, long before we can request it, or demand it, or bargain for it.

Beloved, you have received a fantastic gift. This gift is better than any gift you've ever received because it won't break, it won't rust, it doesn't eat batteries, and it can't be lost. It doesn't matter if you were aware you had it or not. It doesn't matter if your parents acknowledged it on your behalf or didn't. It doesn't matter if you used it for a while and then put it away. The gift is yours because the Gift-Giver, the Holy One, gives it to you.

While this gift is entirely yours, the Gift-Giver doesn't force it
upon you and doesn't require you to open it. I think we can
agree that being forced to love someone isn't love at all.
Instead, God gives the gift to you in love and then longs for
you to let the gift make a difference in your life. It's your
decision if, how, and when you open this gift. Everyone who
gives a gift wants the recipient to enjoy the gift they've
received. God is no different. God wants you to enjoy the
blessings of this incredible gift so that your joy may be
complete, and you may experience abundant life right now.

> *[8]And God is able to provide you with every blessing in abundance,
> so that by always having enough of everything, you may share
> abundantly in every good work (2 Corinthians 9).*
>
> *Jesus said, "[10]I came that they may have life, and have it
> abundantly" (John 10).*
>
> *Jesus said, "[11]I have said these things to you so that my joy may be
> in you, and that your joy may be complete" (John 15).*

It's sometimes difficult for me to sit back and trust that
someone else, including God, can take care of what's
bothering me because I like to be in control of things. I've
found that the more tightly I cling to my way of doing and
being in the world, the more weighed down I am by the
burdens of life. Maybe the same thing happens to you.

Many of us believe that we are supposed to figure things out all by ourselves. Handling everything on our own without asking for or receiving help is the way it's supposed to be, right? Yes, solving problems and making decisions on our own is exciting and invigorating. Yet, over time we may feel isolated and disconnected from others, which can negatively impact our sense of joy and peace. It's hard to be thankful for the experiences and people in your life when you go through life apart from the community.

Beloved, you were created to be in a relationship with the Giver of Gifts and with all of creation. These relationships enable you to be who God made you to be and experience the fullness of all that is yours. That's why God's gift of love overflows with blessings from the One who created you, has loved you from the beginning, and wants only good things for you.

> [17]*Every generous act of giving, with every perfect gift, is from above, coming down from the Father of lights, with whom there is no variation or shadow due to change (James 1).*

The blessings of God's extravagant, encompassing, and empowering gift of love include joy, strength, hope, comfort, interconnectedness, and courage.

The blessing of joy

⁹Therefore my heart is glad, and my soul rejoices; my body also rests secure. ¹⁰For you do not give me up to Sheol or let your faithful one see the Pit. ¹¹You show me the path of life. In your presence there is fullness of joy; in your right hand are pleasures forevermore (Psalm 16).

The blessing of joy is about contentment. It's about focusing on things that matter and letting go of things that don't. It's about accepting that you are enough just as you are and that you have enough no matter what the advertisers tell you. Joy recognizes that you are worthy of love and respect. Accepting this enables you to stop comparing yourself to others so that you can pursue what brings you purpose and meaning, what makes you content, and what gives you joy.

Living in the blessing of joy that God intends for you is about reframing your negative thoughts because they weigh you down and cloud your perspective on who you are and what life is all about. You see, the things you tell yourself shape your behavior and influence how you see the world. When your negative thoughts drive you, your sense of self-worth diminishes, and your confidence wavers. When you reframe your negative thoughts, you can shift from self-criticism to self-acceptance. Rather than complaining, you can give thanks. You can let go of worry about what was or what will be and focus on what is.

Embracing the blessing of joy is about intentionally shifting your perspective from scarcity to abundance, from problems to opportunities, from fear to assurance, from failure to growth, from limitations to freedom, from disappointments to satisfaction, and from regret to contentment. Thus, it transforms how you think about yourself, your past experiences, your current circumstances, and the people who share your life. These shifts help you recognize the positive aspects of your life. You become better equipped to face the challenges that come your way. All this enables you to become more deeply aware of who and what's important.

Beloved, God gives you the blessing of joy. Living in this blessing may not come naturally to you because it's hard work. It requires a deliberate choice to forgo quick fixes and secure solutions. The blessing of joy is about giving thanks for each new day. Embracing who you are and remembering that you are worthy of love, worthy of joy, not because of who you are but because of the One who created you in love and who clothes you with joy.

[13]May the God of hope fill you with all joy and peace in believing, so that you may abound in hope by the power of the Holy Spirit (Romans 15).

[11]You have turned my mourning into dancing; you have taken off my sackcloth and clothed me with joy, [12]so that my soul may praise you and not be silent (Psalm 30).

The blessing of comfort

[4]Rejoice in the Lord always; again, I will say, rejoice. [5]Let your gentleness be known to everyone. The Lord is near. [6]Do not worry about anything, but in everything by prayer and supplication with thanksgiving let your requests be made known to God. [7]And the peace of God, which surpasses all understanding, will guard your hearts and your minds in Christ Jesus (Philippians 4).

"Rejoice in the Lord always, again, I will say rejoice." These words are challenging! What do you mean "rejoice" when my world is falling apart, when I've lost my job, or just learned of a cancer diagnosis? How in the world can anyone expect me to rejoice over the death of a loved one or a devastating catastrophe? It doesn't make rational sense, does it? Yet here are these words in the Christian Bible. Corrie Ten Boom made sense of the words in the passage above when she said, "Worry does not empty tomorrow of its sorrow. It empties today of its strength."[13]

Beloved, we rejoice, not because of what is happening to us or around us. We rejoice because "The Lord is near." It's the nearness of the Holy One that comforts and strengthens us to face our worst fears, our hardest days, and our biggest

---

[13] Corrie Ten Boom, quoted by Carol Kelly-Gangi, editor, A Woman's Book of Inspiration: Quotes of Wisdom and Strength, (New York: Fall River Press, 2017), 36.

disappointments. It's the nearness of the Holy One that enables us to let go of our worry. I know that's easier said than done. I can pray for God to take my troubles, my worries, my fears from me and then turn around and pick them right back up again. I've been on that roller coaster ride many times in my life. Beloved, know that this is not a sign of weakness or a lack of faith. Instead, it's a reminder that I'm not perfect, we're not perfect people.

The gift of prayer

That's why God gives us the gift of prayer. God doesn't need our prayers to provide for us. God doesn't wait for us to pray before God takes action. Instead, prayer is a gift given to us, so we have a tangible way to live with the One who created us and initiated a relationship with us. And so, we are invited to make our requests known to God so we can see that we're not carrying our burdens alone.

As Mother Teresa said, *"Prayer is not asking. Prayer is putting oneself in the hands of God, at his disposition, and listening to his voice in the depths of our hearts."*[14]

---

[14] Mother Teresa, *In My Own Words*, comp. Jose Luis Gonzalez-Balado (Liguori, MO.: Liguori Publications, 1996) 9.

Listening to God's presence in prayer brings us peace and draws us into a deeper experience of the Holy.

Philippians 4 continues:

> [7]*And the peace of God, which surpasses all understanding, will guard your hearts and your minds in Christ Jesus.*

Once more we share in the peace of the Holy One. This peace is bigger than us because it doesn't come from us and it doesn't depend on us. This peace is a gift intended to comfort and strengthen our hearts and our minds

One of my favorite theologians is Leslie Weatherhead. He served as the minister at City Temple in London from 1936–1960. Like most of London, the City Temple was reduced to rubble during World War II and the London Blitz. Weatherhead crafted a series of sermons on understanding the will of God to help the congregation cope as their church and the city crumbled around them. These are published in the book *The Will of God.*[15] I've found his understanding of the will of God helpful in thinking about where God is in the midst of suffering.

---

[15] Leslie D. Weatherhead, *The Will of God*, (New York: Abingdon Press, 1999).

Weatherhead identifies God's will in three ways. First is God's Intentional Will—one of blessing, harmony, balance, and peace in all creation. This is the way that God intended our relationship with the Holy and with each other to be. Next is God's Circumstantial Will, the ways that God works in the midst of the circumstances in our lives in the here and now. Finally, is God's Ultimate Will, Weatherhead explains that this is realized when creation is restored back to God's intention, back to the way God intended things to be from the very beginning.

Beloved, God doesn't cause the bad things that happen to you or those you love, but God works in those hard times and bad situations, in your pain and disappointments, to bring you blessing, restoration, balance, and peace. God does this by putting people in your life who can support you, people who can pray on your behalf when you don't feel like praying, people who can hold your hand when you need the comfort of another person, people who can cry and laugh with you. God meets you where you are and carries you into a new reality, into God's Ultimate Will where blessing, restoration, balance, and peace are renewed.

Receive the blessing below and remember that you are loved, that you have received eternal comfort and good hope from the Holy One, not because of anything that you've done or said, so that you are comforted and strengthened as you face the ups and downs of life.

¹⁶Now may our Lord Jesus Christ himself and God our Father, who loved us and through grace gave us eternal comfort and good hope, ¹⁷comfort your hearts and strengthen them in every good work and word (2 Thessalonians 2).

The blessing of strength

¹⁰Do not fear, for I am with you, do not be afraid, for I am your God; I will strengthen you, I will help you, I will uphold you with my victorious right hand (Isaiah 41).

What frightens you? I was recently driving on a winding two-lane road where many of the curves are blind spots for both lanes. As I was coming around a corner, a large white SUV came around the corner from the opposite direction. It shouldn't have been a problem, except the SUV had crossed over the double yellow center lines and was coming straight at me. It happened so fast that I had no time to blow my horn to alert the driver that I was there. Instead, all I could do was to get out of my lane. I quickly hit my brakes and pulled onto the shoulder while going about 25 mph. The SUV sped passed me in what should have been my lane. I brought my car to a stop and sat on the side of the road for a while. My heart was racing, my body was shaking, and my breathing was rapid. I slowly pulled back onto the road, but after a mile, I pulled over again because I was crying uncontrollably. This frightened me to my core.

Thankfully, my friend called at that moment in response to a message I had left earlier. She could tell I was upset, so she listened as I recalled what had happened earlier and continued talking with me until I settled down. Before we hung up, she prayed with me, which was most helpful. After hanging up with her, I called my husband who listened as I, again, recalled what happened. He spoke words of comfort and assurance. This frightening experience kept my heart rate and breathing accelerated for the rest of the day and the entire next day.

> [29][The LORD] gives power to the faint and strengthens the powerless. [30]Even youths will faint and be weary, and the young will fall exhausted; [31]but those who wait for the LORD shall renew their strength, they shall mount up with wings like eagles, they shall run and not be weary, they shall walk and not faint (Isaiah 40).

Our complicated life gives us opportunities that comfort and strengthen us and opportunities that make us feel weary and powerless. Thankfully, we can turn to the Holy One in the good times as well as the hard times. I've noticed that when things are going well, I am less likely to acknowledge the presence of the Holy One. Instead, I might take credit for what's going well and then pat myself on the back. I suspect that I'm not alone in this behavior. I've found that when I recognize God's presence in the good times, I experience a more profound, longer-lasting sense of joy and excitement.

¹God is our refuge and strength, a very present help in trouble. ²Therefore we will not fear, though the earth should change, though the mountains shake in the heart of the sea; ³though its waters roar and foam, though the mountains tremble with its tumult (Psalm 46).

Beloved, the Holy One promises to be your "refuge and strength, a very present help in trouble." You don't need to face your fears, your adversities, your challenges by yourself. You can lean into the presence of the Holy One to help you overcome whatever is pushing against you. Sometimes, when bad things are happening to us and around us, we may not recognize the presence of the Holy One. Sometimes, we can become so focused on our pain and our hardships that we can't see God at work.

My seminary professor, The Rev. Dr. Tony Everette, coined the word "WIGIAT." This is not a word you'll find in a dictionary and it's really not a word at all. Instead, it is an acronym formed by the first letters of the words in the question: Where is God in all this? Intentionally asking this question, our attention can shift away from our problems to our blessings. When we ask the WIGIAT question, we are expecting God to be present already. This perspective helps us recognize God at work.

Beloved, God is present in the people who show up for you, the people who are helping you, and the people who are sitting with you. God is at work in the helpful actions that you are taking in response to what is happening or that others are taking on your behalf. God is at work in the alternatives that you are thinking about or in the suggestions that are coming your way. When we anticipate the presence of the Holy One, we are more likely to actually recognize and experience that presence.

The presence of the Holy One doesn't mean that everything will always go your way or that your life will be easy and free from pain and suffering. No, as much as we might want it to be, that was never the Lord's promise to you. Instead, the Lord promises to be with you. The Lord promises to strengthen and help you. The Holy One promises to uphold you as you journey through the ups and downs of life.

The blessing of hope

5For God alone my soul waits in silence, for my hope is from him. 6He alone is my rock and my salvation, my fortress; I shall not be shaken. 7On God rests my deliverance and my honor; my mighty rock, my refuge is in God. 8Trust in him at all times, O people; pour out your heart before him; God is a refuge for us (Psalm 62).

The psalmist declares that our hope is a blessing from God who alone is our rock; and the One in whom we can take refuge, the One in whom we can trust, and the One to whom we can pour out our hearts. This means that, even when we feel alone in our struggles, God is with us.

Yet when our lives are complicated and much of it is outside of our control, hope can sometimes be hard to muster. You can hear this in conversations with people who are facing job and economic insecurities, food and housing shortages, and relationship and identity uncertainties. Worrying about our aging parents and our growing children, our own health, and the health of those we love can diminish our sense of hope.

Contrasting optimism and hope, Bruce Marshall explains that optimism has an "expectation that a particular result will occur—that a person will recover from an illness, that we will achieve a specific goal." He stresses that when things don't happen the way we think they should, we are mired in disappointment, which can lead to pessimism. In contrast, he says that "hope looks for possibility in whatever life deals us. Hope does not anticipate a particular outcome but keeps before us the possibility that something useful will come from this." He explains that "hope is more resilient, more enduring, more helpful" than optimism because "hope encourages us to move forward despite the setbacks as we look squarely at the realities that confront us while remaining aware of the possibilities."[16]

---

16 Bruce Marshall, *What we Share: Collected Meditations, Volume 2*, collected and edited by Patricia Frevert, (Boston: Skinner House Books, 2002), 24-26.

So often we think that we have to fix everything that is happening to us and around us by ourselves. We tell ourselves that we need to face our struggles on our own because asking for help might cause people to see us as weak or incapable. This line of thinking can lead to unhealthy ways of being in the world. It's exactly in troubling and uncertain times that we need each other. When we can't think straight, someone else can think on our behalf. When we can't problem-solve, someone else can help us sort out the options.

In speaking about hope-filled people, Joyce Rupp writes:

> *Hope-filled people inspire and boost the enthusiasm of others. With their spiritual roots sunk deep in Abiding Love, they can stand strong in the wild storms of life and not give up hope. Hope-filled people reach out wide and far to receive this empowering strength that comes in many disguises.*[17]

Rupp explains that when faced with suffering and a lack of peace, hope-filled people 'journey inwards to find the Endless Source that feeds the river of love and goodness in our hearts. When we do so, we have the courage to continue hoping in spite of what appears dismal.'[18]

---

[17] Rupp, Joyce, *Constant Hope: Reflections and Meditations to Strengthen the Spirit,* (New London, CT: Twenty-Third Publications, 2019), 20.

[18] Ibid.

Paul explains hope in this way:

24Now hope that is seen is not hope. For who hopes for what is seen? 25But if we hope for what we do not see, we wait for it with patience (Romans 8).

Waiting for hope with patience is a difficult thing to do. We want things, solutions, and answers right now. But that is not how many things work. Sometimes we need to wait years before something we've longed for comes to be.

When my mom was dying under hospice care from advanced lung cancer in 2008, I searched everywhere for a book that would help us navigate this season as a family. I found books by nurses, doctors, and social workers about the hospice experience but couldn't find anything from the perspective of a patient and their family. I promised my mom and myself that I would one day write that book.

Then life got in my way. I maneuvered through the process of settling her estate, served as a pastor in several different congregations, enjoyed time with family and friends, traveled, and returned to the rhythm of my life, all while living with my grief. Every now and then, especially when walking with others through the death of a loved one, I'd be reminded of my promise to one day write the book that I needed and couldn't find.

It took 10 years and several twists and turns before I could write that book. As a pastor, I knew how to write but I didn't know how to publish, so when I heard about the Self-Publishing School, I enrolled. Working with a coach, actually two coaches, and applying what I was learning in the course, I set my mind on actually realizing the promise that I made many years earlier. This filled me with such hope: hope for my family who would have a lasting story about their Grammy and how she was loved and cared for at the end of life; hope for others who would read the book while going through similar experiences as they cared for a loved one; and hope that the book would actually be written, published, and then be added to the enormous collection of books for all time. Hope that the promise I made years before would be fulfilled.

My book, *On the Way: Short Stories and Biblical Reflections on Caring for a Loved One in Hospice,* was published on January 1, 2019. Holding the published book in my hands was a dream come true. Since its publication, hearing how others have experienced peace and hope through their reading of the book continues to fill me with joy.

The Biblical writer of Hebrews assures us that:

> *[19]We have this hope, a sure and steadfast anchor of the soul, a hope that enters the inner shrine behind the curtain, [20]where Jesus, a forerunner on our behalf, has entered (Hebrews 6).*

Beloved, you have received the blessing of hope from the Holy One, the One who is your rock and your refuge. The One in whom you can trust and pour out your heart. This hope is yours with no strings attached. It's a sure and steadfast anchor of your soul because of Jesus who is the forerunner on your behalf. Hold on to this hope when life gets complicated knowing that you are not alone in the struggle.

The blessing of interconnectedness

A deep sense of love and belonging is an irreducible need of all people. We are biologically, cognitively, physically, and spiritually wired to love, to be loved, and to belong. When those needs are not met, we don't function as we were meant to. We break. We fall apart. We numb. We ache. We hurt others. We get sick.[19]

Brené Brown

Life is filled with pain and pleasure, problems and opportunities, cruelty and goodness. As we try to make sense

---

[19] Brené Brown, The Art of Imperfection: Let Go of Who You Think You're Supposed to Be and Embrace Who You Are, (Center City, MN: Hazelden Publishing, 2010), 26.

of it all, our head talk tells us that we must be the best at everything we do, that our success and our happiness depend on what we do, what we accomplish. These messages shape how we approach life and our relationships at home, work, and play.

Beloved, these messages place a heavy burden on you. The reality is that we need each other. We need people in our lives who can support us when we need an extra hand, love us when we feel unlovable, and help us when we feel helpless. God responds to our need for interconnectedness by surrounding us with a great cloud of witnesses.

In my last semester of seminary, I witnessed a murder near the seminary campus. It was springtime, about 6:00 p.m. As I was walking across campus to the apartment of two of my classmates, a young man and young woman crossed my path. We acknowledged each other with the customary head nod and exchanged a quick "hello." About the time they passed by me, someone jumped out from behind a bush and started shooting. I stepped back behind a car. The young woman started screaming and ran to stand near a fence. I motioned for her to get down and to be quiet so the shooter wouldn't shoot her, too. While all of this was happening, the young man fell to the ground. As soon as the shooting stopped, I ran toward the man who was bleeding on the road. The shooter was still standing over him and, thankfully, took off running as I approached.

Gunshots were common in the neighborhood that surrounded the campus, but I never felt unsafe. Because we were used to hearing gunshots, my colleagues, standing outside their apartments didn't react, so I yelled for them to call 911. I sat down on the street and cradled the young man in my lap as he was bleeding on the road. The young woman, his sister, was there with me. Through her tears, she indicated that they were walking home and that their mother worked at the elementary school across the street. Several classmates hurried to get their mother.

Once the emergency responders arrived, they moved the young man to the ambulance. A classmate drove the mother to the hospital where they learned that the young man died on the way. The police who were investigating asked me and the young woman a lot of questions on the scene and then indicated that we needed to go to the police station to make a full report. Even though we had been sitting side-by-side for hours, the police wouldn't let us ride together. The young woman was terrified of riding in the back of a police car and refused to go. I stressed that we needed to do this so the police could find the person who shot her brother. Reluctantly she consented so I asked one of my classmates to ride in the car with her and another to ride with me.

The police kept us separate at the station. I was so worried about this frightened young woman who had just witnessed her brother being shot and who had been shot at herself. Now, she was all alone at the police station. By the time I finished giving my statement, she was gone. The officer said that a family member came to pick her up. Another classmate came to the police station to pick up my classmate and me.

When we got back to the seminary campus, we saw that the lights were on in the seminary chapel, so we went there. We could hear the music and singing as we approached. To my surprise, the chapel was filled with people from the neighborhood, students, faculty, and staff. I was overwhelmed by the outpouring of support and compassion shown to me that night and in the days and weeks that followed. Being part of the seminary community got me through this ordeal. I needed them to walk with me, talk with me, cry with me, and comfort me. They were strong when I couldn't be strong.

To worship God is nothing other than to serve other people. It does not need rosaries, prayer carpets, or robes. All peoples are members of the same body, created from one essence. If fate brings suffering to one member the others cannot stay at rest.[20]

[1]Therefore, since we are surrounded by so great a cloud of witnesses, let us also lay aside every weight and the sin that clings so closely, and let us run with perseverance the race that is set before us, [2]looking to Jesus the pioneer and perfecter of our faith, who for the

---

[20] Saadi Shirazi, *Singing the Living Tradition*, (Boston: Unitarian Universalist Association, 1994), 609.

sake of the joy that was set before him endured the cross, disregarding its shame, and has taken his seat at the right hand of the throne of God (Hebrews 12).

Making your way through a difficult time is made easier when you are surrounded by a nurturing community, a great cloud of witnesses. Communities come in all shapes and sizes. It can be in the form of your family or among your colleagues. Your friends, members of your exercise class, or your book club can be a nurturing community for you. You might experience community with your neighbors or in your faith congregation.

Many years ago, my husband and I attended a marriage enrichment retreat with five other couples. We all had children at home, worked full-time jobs, and most of us were from the same faith community. As we talked about our marriages, we realized that what most of us longed for was having fun times with other adults. At the end of the retreat, we decided that we'd get together once a month, at each other's homes, for fun and fellowship. Together, over more than 10 years, this nurturing community supported one another as our children grew up and as we changed jobs, moved, faced illnesses, and grieved the death of parents.

Beloved, you are surrounded by a great cloud of witnesses. Some have gone before you in death and others walk alongside you now. This great cloud of witnesses shows up when you need them. They are the ones who cry when your tears have run dry. They are the ones who support you when life gets hard. They are the ones who laugh with you. They enjoy being in your presence. They accept you just as you are and encourage you to be the best that you can be. This great cloud of witnesses is God's gift to and for you so you don't do life alone.

The blessing of courage

With faith to face our challenges, with love that casts out fear, and with hope to trust tomorrow, we accept this day as the gift it is, a reason for rejoicing.[21]

Gary Knowalski

Riding the roller coaster of life requires courage. Courage to pursue our passions, face the obstacles that come our way. Courage to learn new things and live in relationship with someone. Courage to be yourself, to love and care for others, and courage to take risks.

After pursuing a master's in adult education, I was launched into the corporate world of training and development. I

---

[21] Gary Knowalski, *Lifting Our Voices: Readings in the Living Tradition*, (Boston: Unitarian Universalist Association, 2015) 84.

found this career, still in education and now working with adults, to be very enjoyable.

At the same time, I was busy raising our two daughters, volunteering as a Girl Scout leader, and serving in my faith community. Eventually, several of my colleagues started telling me that they thought I was being called into the ministry. However, I felt comfortable where I was. I argued that the 3,500 employees whom I interacted with in training and development were enough ministry for me. One day, one of the supervisors in the organization told me that he'd been praying for me and that he believed God was indeed calling me to ministry. He asked that I also pray about this.

The notion of leaving a secure and enjoyable position to go to seminary was more than I could wrap my head around. Our daughters were both in college and my husband and I were enjoying the empty nest. Surely, God wasn't calling me to change everything. I was participating in a Bible study at church and we were looking at the LORD's call to Samuel (1 Samuel 3). This got me thinking, if God called a child, maybe God was calling me too. Maybe I just needed the courage to trust that God might be up to something new.

On my way home from the study, I used the words of Samuel to shape my prayer: "Speak Lord for your servant is listening." I asked God to show me in a clear and tangible way that a call to attend seminary was what God wanted me to do and not just the idea of a few friends and colleagues. A deep sense of peace filled my heart and mind. Several days later, while we were in worship, I was listening to the anthem by the choir. They were singing one of my Dad's favorite hymns, "Joyful, Joyful, We Adore Thee." This hymn always made me think of my Dad who died in 1983. As I sat there listening, with my eyes closed, I heard my Dad's voice say, "God says yes." This took my breath away and brought tears to my eyes.

On the way out, I asked my pastor if he had some time for us to chat that week because I thought I was being called to attend seminary. He smiled broadly and invited me to lunch. As I explained the comments made by my co-workers, shared my prayer after Bible study, and recalled what happened in worship, my pastor said, "You asked God to give you a sign and I think you received a clear answer. What are you going to do about it?" I promised to continue praying about it and asked that he pray for me.

I headed home to talk with my husband about everything. Not long after getting home, my phone rang. It was the Assistant to the Bishop. She indicated that she'd received a call from my pastor and thought that it would be good for us to talk. Next thing I knew I was filling out the application to seminary, completing financial aid documents, giving notice at work, and enrolling in seminary. That was in 2002. Going to seminary was not easy. It took every ounce of courage I could muster.

The seminary I attended was three hours away from my home. I commuted back to campus every Sunday afternoon, lived on campus during the week, and then commuted home on Fridays for three years. I vividly remember the difficult drive back to the campus. I loved going to seminary but being away from my husband and family during the week was extremely difficult. Some Sunday afternoons, I was so upset that I called one of my classmates to talk me into actually returning to the dorm for the next week of classes.

One day, while reading my Bible, I stumbled upon this verse and it immediately became one of my favorite passages:

> *21 And when you turn to the right or when you turn to the left, your ears shall hear a word behind you, saying, "This is the way; walk in it." (Isaiah 30).*

Unsure about what God was up to in my life and where my seminary education would take me, this verse gave me the courage to keep walking and trusting that God was doing something in my life. I wasn't always sure what it was, but I trusted that God was up to something.

Beloved, as you look to the right and to the left, I pray that you will hear the Lord encourage you saying, "This is the way, walk in it."

Summary

The extravagant, encompassing, and empowering gift of God's love is yours. It's yours already. God gave you this gift so that your joy may be complete. You can leave this gift on a shelf, you can ignore it, or you can open it and experience the blessings that you've received.

The blessings of joy, comfort, strength, hope, interconnectedness, and courage are there to support you on the roller coaster we call life. Receiving the blessings of God enables you to experience joy amid sorrow and comfort in the face of struggles. They strengthen you when you feel weak and provide hope amid despair. These blessings foster a sense of connectedness when you feel alone and courage when challenges come your way. Together, they enable you to live in the fullness of all that God desires for you and be the best you that you can be.

These blessings permeate every aspect of your life, every aspect of our shared experiences. They are the basis on which we can thrive in life and grow in love for one another and for the Holy One who bestows these gifts. Whether you are a person of a particular faith tradition or someone who claims no religious affiliation, these blessings are yours because of the expansive and abundant love that God showers upon all of creation.

Questions to ponder

- Which of these blessings most resonate with you and why?

- Which blessings do you most long for right now?

- How can you go about cultivating this blessing in your life?

- What questions, thoughts, and concerns do you have about this chapter?

CHAPTER 11

Living in the Gift of God's Love

---

*Anything can become a spiritual practice once you
are willing to approach it that way—once you let it bring
you to your knees and show you what is real, including
who you really are, who other people are, and how
near God can be when you have lost your way.*[22]

Barbara Brown Taylor

We've established that God's love for us is a gift given
without expectation. This gift reveals that God's love is
extravagant, encompassing, and empowering. It includes the
attributes of acceptance, compassion, inclusion, and peace,
and the blessings of joy, comfort, strength, hope,

---

[22] Barbara Brown Taylor, *An Altar in the World: A Geography of Faith*, (New York:
HarperOne, 2010), 81.

interconnectedness, and courage. Now, we'll explore what living in God's gift of love is all about.

Wrapped in the quilt of God's love sets you free to live. You need not worry about whether or not you are loved by God, if you are saved, or where you will spend eternity. God's action in raising Jesus from the dead ensures that all is well with you. Despite the messages you may hear, God doesn't need you to do anything or say anything to receive the blessings of God's unconditional, expansive, and eternal love.

Yes, Beloved, this may sound too good to be true. That is what some well-meaning Christians want you to believe. They promote that a person needs to accept Jesus as their personal Lord and Savior in order to be saved, that a person needs to do certain things and believe in certain ways to be loved by God. For some, this way of thinking about their relationship with God is comforting because it means that there are clear expectations for everyone.

Promoting rules and expectations about how a person can receive God's love can have a negative effect on a person's physical, cognitive, emotional, and spiritual well-being. Stressing over whether or not you've been good enough for God to love you can diminish your joy. Wondering if you'll be forgiven for something that you've done or not done can cause you to be uncomfortable in your relationship with others and with God. Believing that you must adhere to certain doctrines and practices in order to be saved can cause you to doubt your goodness and question your worthiness of God's love.

Worrying about whether you've said or done the right things can consume your spirit and reduce your ability to live with hope. When you feel unlovable, you might withdraw from relationships and feel disconnected from God and others. When you live in fear because you're afraid that you won't measure up to what God expects, your ability to face life courageously is undermined. Beloved, none of this is what God wants for you.

The truth is that God's unconditional, abundant, and undeniable love is yours. While it might sound too good to be true, you can trust that it is true. God really does love you! Has loved you from the beginning and will continue to love you for all the tomorrows to come. Not because of what you do or say, its yours because of the One who embraces you in love.

One of the first things Jesus did in his public ministry was go to the synagogue. There he proclaimed these words (based on Isaiah 61):

> *[18]The Spirit of the Lord is upon me, because he has anointed me to bring good news to the poor. He has sent me to proclaim release to the captives and recovery of sight to the blind, to let the oppressed go free, [19]to proclaim the year of the Lord's favor." [20]And he rolled up the scroll, gave it back to the attendant, and sat down. The eyes of*

all in the synagogue were fixed on him. ²¹*Then he began to say to them, "Today this scripture has been fulfilled in your hearing (Luke 4).*

Jesus understood that his mission was based on action, not just any kind of action, but action that liberates, frees, restores, heals, and reconciles. He didn't place conditions on these actions or indicate that they would only apply if someone said or did something first. No, just as God is the initiator of love and the initiator of blessings, Jesus initiates action that embraces everyone. Reading from the scroll of Isaiah, Jesus announced that he fulfills all that has been promised.

We are free, Beloved, not because of anything that we've said or done. We're free because we've been made free.

³⁶So if the Son makes you free, you will be free indeed (John 8).

We're free because we are yoked to Jesus. A yoke was made of wood and carved to fit the neck and shoulders of the animal to prevent pain and discomfort while hauling a heavy load. Often times one animal would be yoked to another to share the burden. Jesus invites us:

²⁸Come to me, all you that are weary and are carrying heavy burdens, and I will give you rest. ²⁹Take my yoke upon you and

learn from me; for I am gentle and humble in heart, and you will find rest for your souls. [30]For my yoke is easy, and my burden is light (Matthew 11).

We all carry heavy burdens, we're weary from the struggles in this life, so out of great compassion, Jesus says, come to me. He doesn't put any conditions on this invitation. He doesn't say only after you've accepted me can you come to me. He doesn't say, when you have your life under control, then you can come to me. No, Jesus says, "Come to me and I will give you rest." Being yoked to Jesus means that you aren't expected to carry the heavy burdens by yourself. Jesus assures you that he carries the burden with you and that in God you will find rest for your soul.

We're free because we are yoked to Jesus, who is the pioneer and perfecter of our faith.

Therefore, since we are surrounded by so great a cloud of witnesses, let us also lay aside every weight and the sin that clings so closely, and let us run with perseverance the race that is set before us, [2] looking to Jesus the pioneer and perfecter of our faith, who for the sake of the joy that was set before him endured the cross, disregarding its shame, and has taken his seat at the right hand of the throne of God (Hebrews 12:1–2).

Being yoked to Jesus is about being gathered within the embrace of his faithfulness. Jesus initiates and perfects our faith. He establishes and completes our faith.

Faith is not adhering to a set of doctrines; it's not making a statement of belief. Here are two definitions of faith that influence my understanding.

- *Martin Luther—Faith is a living, daring confidence in God's grace, so sure and certain that a man could stake his life on it a thousand times.*[23]

- *Richard Rohr—Faith at its essential core is accepting that you are accepted! We cannot deeply know ourselves without knowing the One who made us, and we cannot fully accept ourselves without accepting God's radical acceptance of every part of us.*[24]

Beloved, Jesus was the only faithful one. No one else is faithful. We may claim to have faith, but as soon as something happens, we doubt that faith. Wavering between

---

[23] Martin Luther, *Preface to the Letter of St. Paul to the Romans*, retrieved April 8, 2020, from https://www.ccel.org/l/luther/romans/pref_romans.html

[24] Richard Rohr, The Universal Christ: How a Forgotten Reality Can Change Everything We See, Hope For, and Believe, (New York: Convergent Books, 2019), 29.

faith and doubt is not about being inherently sinful; it's about being imperfect. Doubting is not a sign of a lack of faith. Instead, it's a normal response when faced with uncertain times and circumstances. Thankfully, our relationship with the Holy One doesn't depend on our own faith. Instead, we are yoked to Jesus and share in his faith which enables us to trust in his faithfulness rather than our own.

I'm drawn to the quote below because it reminds me that God is the only perfect one:

There is no perfect life, no perfect job, no perfect childhood, no perfect marriage, and no perfect set of people who will always do what we expect them to do. What we have is a perfect God who is able to lead us through this imperfect life with unfailing strength, incomparable wisdom, and infinite love.[25]

Faith is falling into the net of God's extravagant, encompassing, and empowering love. It's being grasped by the God who adores you and who accepts you just as you are. God bestows compassion on you in every moment of every day. God has redeemed you, called you by name, and claimed you as God's own. You are precious in God's sight and loved

---

[25] Unknown. I came across it at https://debbiebertrand.blogspot.com/2019/11/sayings-to-ponder.html. It was accessed on April 11, 2020.

completely. God chooses you and includes you in the family of God because it is God's good pleasure to do lavish us with glorious grace. God establishes peace between us and among us. Everything else may come tumbling down around us but God's steadfast love will not depart, and the covenant of peace will never fail.

Even so, our lives won't be easy or free from suffering and pain. We still live in an imperfect world filled with imperfect people, us included. God's acceptance, compassion, inclusion, and peace are about God's commitment to us, not our commitment to God. Because of God's commitment to restoring all of creation to the Creator, we need not fear what will happen to us when we die; instead, we can focus on living in the here and now. We can focus on being the person God creates us to be.

A three-fold mindset for living in the gift of God's love

Living in the blessings of God's love is about living with intention, humility, and balance. Each of these attitudes can have a positive impact on our lives and our relationships with the Holy One and each other. Together they can strengthen our capacity to enjoy life and the people who share it with us. When we engage intention, humility, and balance, we will experience the fullness of God's extravagant, encompassing, and empowering love.

Living with intention

One way that we live with intention is by waking up every day and asking, Where is God in all this? When you ask the WIGIAT question, you ignite your senses to see God at work. Moving through your day, expecting God to be present in all that you do, and say enables you to see the goodness and blessings in your life. When we intentionally make space for God, we are more likely to experience the blessings that flow from God's great love. Living with intention is about choosing joy over sorrow, comfort over pain, strength over weakness, hope over despair, interconnectedness over isolation, and courage over fear. We live with intention by extending compassion to those around us rather than reacting to people in ways that cause harm. We can do this by reframing our negative thoughts and actions into thoughts that reflect patience and understanding and actions that acknowledge the goodness of others.

Living with humility

Adopting the mindset of humility starts with accepting who you are—your strengths and your weaknesses, your challenges and your successes, your hopes and your fears—and then making space for others to be who they are. Heather Plett explains what it means to hold space for another person like this:

It means that we are willing to walk alongside another person in whatever journey they're on without judging them, making them feel inadequate, trying to fix them, or trying to impact the outcome. When we hold space for other people, we open our hearts, our unconditional support, and let go of judgment and control.[26]

Sometimes people think that showing humility is a sign of weakness, a sign that someone lacks confidence. On the contrary, humility is a demonstration of strength. It's about asking for what you need, saying no when you need or want to, apologizing when you've done something wrong, and owning your own feelings, thoughts, and actions. We show humility by acknowledging the good that others do and stepping aside so someone else can step forward.

Rumi, the 13th century Persian poet, Islamic scholar, and Sufi mystic, describes an approach to living with humility amid the ups and downs of life in this poem:

This being human is a guest house.
Every morning a new arrival.
A joy, a depression, a meanness,

---

[26] Heather Plett, What it means to "hold space" for people, plus eight tips on how to do it well, Retrieved February 5, 2020, from https://heatherplett.com/2015/03/hold-space/.

some momentary awareness comes
as an unexpected visitor.

Welcome and entertain them all!
Even if they're a crowd of sorrows,
who violently sweep your house
empty of its furniture,
still, treat each guest honorably.
He may be clearing you out
for some new delight.

The dark thought, the shame, the malice,
meet them at the door laughing,
and invite them in. Be grateful for whoever comes,
because each has been sent
as a guide from beyond.[27]

Living with balance

*Life is about balance. You don't always need to be getting
stuff done. Sometimes it's perfectly okay, and absolutely
necessary, to shut down, kick back, and do nothing.*

Lori Deschene

---

[27] Jalaluddin Rumi, *Rumi: Selected Poems*, trans Coleman Barks with John Moynce,
A. J. Arberry, Reynold Nicholson (Penguin Books, 2004).

Life places many expectations and responsibilities on us. Each day we wear many hats and are different things to different people. Sometimes these are in competition with each other for our attention. We're pulled in different directions and need to juggle diverse priorities, often requiring us to make quick adjustments along the way. There is no doubt that all this juggling makes it challenging to find balance.

Sometimes the intensity of life is more than we can manage. Rather than hitting the pause button on our lives so we can catch our breath, we tend to push forward as best we can.

God doesn't intend for you to wear yourself out being everything to everybody. Even God took time to rest, modeling the best way we can seek balance in our life: keeping the Sabbath. Each of the Gospels tell us that Jesus went away to pray. In the Christian tradition, this is most often associated with going to church on Sundays and dedicating Sundays to family time. In the Jewish tradition, Sabbath is honored from sundown on Friday until sunset on Saturday. Like the Christian tradition, our Jewish sisters and brothers devote their Sabbath time to worship and family. Unfortunately, our Holy Days can be as busy or busier than the other days in the week. So maybe they aren't really Sabbath days.

Beloved, Sabbath is a gift that God gives to us, not because God needs it, but because we need it. We need moments of rest and renewal. It's when we run ourselves ragged that our health declines, our relationships suffer, and our ability to problem-solve and interact well with others is diminished. So often we feel guilty for taking time for ourselves, we believe that we're being selfish or rude when we say "no" to things. This response isn't helpful. Remember, God has given the gift of Sabbath for our benefit so that we can live full and abundant lives.

Sabbath-keeping can happen any day of the week and at any time of the day. Sometimes it's grabbing an hour to soak in the tub or take a walk around the park. Sometimes it's curling up to read a new book or spending some time exercising. Sabbath-keeping can happen in your quiet alone time and in your time with friends and family. The key to Sabbath-keeping is finding what nourishes you, what gives you rest, and what restores your spirit.

Cultivating a sense of balance takes focus and attention. You will always have commitments and expectations, choices and opportunities; therefore, deliberately pausing to catch your breath will enable you to make informed choices as you strive for balance.

Living in God's love sets us free

Living in the blessings of God's love with intention, humility, and balance empowers you to live a more peaceful life, a life where relationships matter more than accomplishments and uniqueness matters more than conformity. Living in the blessings of God's love sets you free to embrace paradox, mystery, and spiritual practices that will nourish you. Living in the blessings of God's love enables you to accept yourself and others as beloved children of God.

Embracing the paradox of both/and

One of the concepts that informs my faith is the notion of paradox. The Merriam-Webster dictionary defines paradox as "a statement that is seemingly contradictory or opposed to common sense and yet is perhaps true."[28] The paradox that most influences our society is an either/or understanding of the world. Applying either/or thinking to people goes like this: a person is either bad or good, saved or lost, trustworthy or immoral, forgiven or damned. Categorizing people using the dichotomy of either/or is misguided. Rarely is someone or something completely good or bad. There are nuances in the human spirit that make either/or thinking impractical and disrespectful. Either/or thinking fails to recognize the complexity of humanity and the intricacies of the world in which we live.

---

[28] Merriam-Webster.com s.v. "paradox," accessed April 3, 2020 https://www.merriam-webster.com/dictionary/paradox

Sometimes either/or thinking is applied to God by thinking of God as either punishing or forgiving, angry or loving, compassionate or cruel. This way of thinking doesn't recognize the bigness of God's embrace. It doesn't acknowledge the depth of God's commitment to humanity. It doesn't capture the nuances in God's love story or the way God continues to be active in the world.

We can challenge either/or thinking by adopting a both/and way of understanding. When we consider both/and, we acknowledge that God is both hidden and present, there is both death and resurrection, suffering and peace, illness and healing. People are both sinners, unable to love God with all our heart, soul, mind, and strength and saints, completely forgiven and loved by God. This paradox captures the notion of the already and not yet. We already experience the love of God in our lives right now and we wait for God's promises to be fulfilled.

Embracing the paradox of both/and sets us free to live. It can take away our compulsion to separate people and situations into either/or groups. It eliminates our anxiety about whether we are in or out, whether we are accepted or rejected. Rather than worrying about the either/or's, we can celebrate that God loves us completely and wants us to live in hope through the ups and downs of life.

Embracing the both/and paradox encompasses the fullness of who God is and who we are. Yes, we experience death because our bodies are fragile and resurrection, new life, to come. Death and resurrection are part of our everyday lives as we move from season to season, and as our lives change over time. Yes, suffering exists, and we can rest in the assurance that God is with us in suffering. Yes, people get sick, and people experience healing; sometimes that happens in life, and other times it happens in death. By their seemingly contradictory nature, paradoxes can be challenging to explain. That's why embracing mystery is necessary.

Embracing mystery

Mystery is at the heart of everything we say and do when it comes to our relationship with the Holy One, because this relationship is beyond our human understanding.

Maybe you've been or are still part of a community that expects everything you do, believe, or think to fit neatly into a tidy and logical box. Any questions, doubts, or differences of opinion are frowned upon and pushed aside. You've learned that everything has a place and that there's a logical explanation for everything that happens. All that's needed is trust.

The problem with this is that it doesn't allow space for mystery. Doctrines don't always fit together neatly. Scriptures don't always make sense. Things don't always happen for a reason. Faith communities, families, and society at large don't always get along and don't always do the right thing.

Each of us has spiritual, family, and cultural narratives that shape how we experience the world around us. We filter everything that happens to us and around us through these narratives. When they don't make sense or don't fit neatly into what we've come to accept, we might discover that we're in a thin place.

The term, thin place, originated in Celtic Christianity. The ancient Celts believed that every aspect of life is infused with the Divine. They thought that there are locations and days of the year where the veil between the physical world and the spiritual realm opens up, giving us a glimpse into the sacred space. Lacy Clark Ellman defines a thin place this way:

> *A thin place is a term used for millennia to describe a place in time where the space between heaven and earth grows thin and the Sacred and the secular seem to meet.*[29]

Thin places give us opportunities to experience things differently. When we realize that we are no longer tied to former ways of thinking and being in the world, we can

---

[29] Lacy Clark Ellman, asacredjourney.net, retrieved February 7, 2020 from asacredjourney.net., https://www.asacredjourney.net/thin-places/.

redefine who we are and how we want our lives to move forward. A thin place can touch us deep within and draw us into tangible experiences with the Divine. In this thin place, we encounter the mystery of the Holy One.

Thin places appear inside and outside of particular faith communities or spiritual paths. Rituals, liturgies, and practices of a faith community or spiritual path can create a thin place where an encounter with the Divine is possible. A thin place might be listening to or singing a song and joining with others in a drumming circle. We can experience a thin place while sitting around a fire and watching the flames flicker. Participating in a task that benefits others or linking arms to work for justice and peace can create a thin place.

Within the Christian tradition, Holy Baptism and Holy Communion can be places that create a thin place. In baptism, the one being baptized experiences the tangible and visible gift of God's extravagant, encompassing, and empowering love. This love embraces the baptized forever. Everyone who witnesses the baptism remembers their baptism in ways that create a thin place. It is this thin place that reveals God as the initiator and perfecter of faith. How this happens remains a mystery.

Receiving Holy Communion can be another example of a thin place. The action of receiving bread and wine in the community opens up this space. I've often felt most connected to my deceased parents during communion. For some, heaven and earth join together for a few minutes as the community shares in this meal. While denominations describe what happens in Holy Communion in different ways, we don't know how the Divine comes to us. The best that we can do is acknowledge and give thanks for the mystery of God's presence.

Embracing mystery enables us to express our doubts and ask hard questions. We can explore new possibilities and rethink beliefs that we've followed blindly. Embracing mystery helps us unleash our capacity to create something new while remaining open to what lies ahead. By embracing mystery, we can share in the story of God's love that is unfolding within us, among us, and all around us.

Mystery accepts that the ways of God are beyond our understanding. Scholars, theologians, pastors, rabbis, imams, preachers, teachers, and adherents of every faith tradition and spiritual experience spend much time trying to understand the nature, words, and actions of the Holy One. I've attempted to do that in this book.

The truth is that our words and our understandings will always fall short. I'm sure that mine have. That's okay. You may not agree with everything I've included in this book, and I'm okay with that. God encounters each of us differently, which is part of the mystery of God. I consider it a privilege to share my thoughts with you and hope that someday we can be in conversation together. This quote by Brian Zahnd reflects my thoughts:

> *We all make errors in our theology; you and me both. So, my recommendation is to err on the side of love. Why? Because . . . God is not doctrine. God is not denomination. God is not war. God is not law. God is not hate. God is not hell. God is Love.*[30]

Embracing mystery is about allowing ourselves to be comfortable with what we don't know and don't understand, so that new connections, new understandings can come into being.

Embracing mystery is about recognizing that God is bigger than any of us can ever understand. However, this needn't stop us from seeking a deeper understanding and closer relationship with the Holy One, who is known by many names, if that is what we desire. By making space for mystery, we open ourselves to an experience with Divine Love that is both unique and personal, expansive and corporate, and motivated by God's love for all of humanity and the created world. We can deepen our experience of the mysteries of

---

[30] Brian Zahnd, brianzahnd.com, retrieved on February 5, 2020, from twitter.com/brianzahnd,
https://twitter.com/brianzahnd/status/1012201620216696833?lang=en.

God and God's relationship with creation through the use of spiritual practices.

Embracing spiritual practices that nourish you

Each one of us has a unique experience in this world and in our relationship with the Divine; therefore, we are drawn to different spiritual practices. Embracing spiritual practices involves exploring the possibilities until you find the ones that resonate with you.

Joan Tollifson explains it this way:

> *There is no one-size-fits-all spiritual practice or pointer. One person will gravitate to a highly structured approach, another to an approach that is more open and spontaneous. For some, meditating daily on a schedule or practicing with a group may be essential. For others, these activities just get in the way. What we need in one moment may be different from what we need in another moment. There is no one right way. This universe is magnificently diverse and playful.[31]*

---

[31] Joan Tollifson, *Nothing to Grasp*, (Salisbury: United Kingdom: Non-Duality Press), 137.

Once you start with a practice, it may take a while before you become comfortable. It might be helpful to talk with others who use the practice or do some research to learn the ins and outs of the practice. Be kind to yourself and take time to learn. Rarely is there a right or wrong way to apply a spiritual practice, so don't hesitate to make adjustments until you find what works best for you.

Sue Monk Kidd encourages us in this way:

> *"You create a path of your own by looking within yourself and listening to your soul, cultivating your own ways of experiencing the sacred and then practicing it. Practicing until you make it a song that sings you."*[32]

Just about anything you do can become a spiritual practice. You can engage in them at any time and in any place. When standing in line, driving, or completing a household task, you can intentionally acknowledge the presence of the Divine. You can pray for the people in line with you or driving beside you. You can give thanks for them and ask that they be kept safe from harm. As you complete household chores, you can speak a blessing for your family members and pray for them as you move from room to room. Embrace the mystery and

---

[32] Sue Monk Kidd, *Dance of the Dissident Daughter: A Woman's Journey from Christian Tradition to the Sacred Feminine.* (New York: HarperOne, 1996), 192.

use your imagination as you incorporate spiritual practices into your life.

Many spiritual practices are available; some are described here:

Art—creativity gives you many ways to experience the Holy. Drawing or painting a picture, coloring, making a collage, cross-stitching, quilting, knitting, crocheting, making jewelry, assembling a puzzle, or using your hands to complete other creative projects. These projects give you opportunities to making something new from the raw materials of your craft.

Journaling—Writing poetry, reflecting about your day, making a list of what you're thankful for each day, making notes on what you're thinking about and how you're feeling, and recording where you've seen God throughout your day. These practices can help you express your experience with God through the written word.

Labyrinth walking—Walking and praying a labyrinth is an ancient spiritual practice. While a labyrinth might look like a maze, it isn't. Mazes have dead ends that require the walker to turn around and go another direction. Labyrinths are a circular path with no dead ends. The walker follows the path into the center and then retraces the path until they return to the place where they started. There are many different ways to walk and pray a labyrinth. Typically, a person pauses at the entrance to identify what they will be praying about before starting the path. The path leading into the center is an opportunity to let go of what's troubling them. Once in the center, the walker can pause again to seek the wisdom and guidance of the Holy One. The path leading away from the center is an opportunity to ask the Holy One to fill you with what you need to carry on. Many churches and communities now include labyrinths on their grounds. A quick internet search will help you find one near you.

Lectio Divina—This is a Latin phrase that literally means divine reading. It's an ancient practice of dwelling in the words of scripture. The scripture can be the words of the Old and New Testaments, the Quran, or other writings that are important to you. In Lectio Divina, you read the passage four times, giving you an opportunity to think deeply and respond thoughtfully to what's been read. In the first reading, listen carefully for words or phrases that resonate with you. In the second reading, think about what the Holy One is saying to you through the word or phrase you focused on during the first reading. After the third reading, think about how the Holy One is calling you to respond to what you've read. Is there something you are being called to do as a result of this text? Following the fourth reading, spend some time in silent contemplation as you rest in the presence of the Holy One.

Meditation—The process of meditating is about being still as you focus on your breathing and let your mind go free. There is nothing that you need to do or say; there is no right or wrong way to meditate, no good or bad meditation. Some people like to use guided meditations, either listened to through an app or read in a book, while others are comfortable simply sitting still and being silent. Meditation is about being present in the moment. It's about letting your breathing be your anchor so you can remain in the here and now on purpose and without judgment. You can try meditation by following these steps: take a seat any way you'd like in a place that is quiet and calm; light a candle to establish that this time and place are important; set a reasonable timer—one minute, three minutes, five minutes—and build up from there; follow the sensation of your breath as you slowly breathe in and out; notice when your mind has wandered and then return to the anchor of your breath; be kind to yourself by suspending judgment and gently returning to the present. When you're ready, open your eyes and notice how your body, thoughts, and emotions are feeling. If you'd like, note this in your journal.

Music—Music in all forms has a way of touching us deeply. Whether or not you're singing, listening to music, dancing, composing, or playing an instrument, music can generate a spiritual experience.

Nature—Spending time in nature can be a refreshing spiritual practice. To be immersed in the sacred, you can take a walk or run, go on a hike, ride a bike, skate, play a sport, have a picnic, go to the beach, garden and do yard work, or look at butterflies, birds, and other animals. As you enjoy the beauty of creation, consider the ways that God shows up.

Prayer—There are many different ways to pray. You can use prayer books to shape your prayers or pray spontaneously. Your prayers can be spoken aloud or offered in silence. We can bring our own needs and concerns to God in prayer while expressing gratitude for the blessings that we've received. Intercessory prayer is what we do when we intercede on behalf of others. Contemplative prayer is about welcoming the presence of the Holy One and then resting in that presence in silence while listening deeply to God. There are no right or wrong ways to pray. Prayer is listening to the Holy One, sometimes that includes talking, but often it's simply listening.

Pilgrimage—Pilgrimages are unique opportunities to go away and be immersed in an experience. Oftentimes, people participate in pilgrimages with other people but sometimes a solitary experience is desired. You might do a pilgrimage to a Holy site far away from your home, visit a place nearby, or spend time on a hike, at the mountains, beach, or a park. Planning and preparing for a pilgrimage can help to provide insight and readiness for what you might see or do. Some pilgrimages can take months or weeks to complete while others can be last a weekend or just a day or two. Carving out time and resources for a pilgrimage takes focus and commitment.

Retreats—Taking intentional time away can have lots of benefits. You can participate in planned retreats facilitated by someone or plan your own retreat where you set the pace and determine how you will spend the time. Retreats can happen in places like camps, retreat centers, or any place where you can be refreshed. You can pause during a busy day to retreat from the chaos of your life. That might be taking a walk, sitting in a quiet place, taking a bubble bath, or spending time with a friend. Retreats are not about how much time you spend or where you go, it's about the quality of time you devote to your time apart, how you spend the time, and what you take away from your time apart.

Spiritual companioning—Life can be difficult for everyone, especially if we try to go it alone. In the midst of the ups and downs and twists and turns of life our relationship with God can suffer. We can get so wrapped up in our own thoughts that we lose sight of a bigger more life-giving narrative. We can get bogged down in what we're expected to do and how we're expected to be in this world that we lose sight of who we are. If you are an active participant in a faith community, you might discover that you're so busy doing stuff in the faith community that you don't have time to simply be in the faith community. To combat this, you can engage in spiritual companioning, a practice of intentionally seeking a deeper understanding of God's presence in your life. Sometimes spiritual companioning happens within a small group of people who want to gain insight from one another as they reflect on their experiences in life while wondering where God is in the midst of it all. In a spiritual companion group, each person has the opportunity to share a thought, concern, or question about what is happening in their lives and in their relationship with the Holy One. Other members of the group listen deeply and prayerfully. After a time of silence, the other members might ask questions or offer observations intended to help the person who shared go deeper into their thoughts. Together the group seeks to answer the question, where is God in all this? Some people prefer a one-to-one conversation with a spiritual companion to explore more intimately where God is in the midst of like. Spiritual companioning is about pausing for a while and intentionally tending to our relationship with the Holy One that can be done in a small group environment and in one-to-one conversations.

Worship—Like the other spiritual practices described in this section, worship also comes in different forms. Worship can take place in sanctuaries, community centers, outdoors, and in your own home. You can set up a home altar where you can offer worship that is meaningful to you. Corporate worship is about gathering with others to share in a common experience of worshipping the Holy One. This might include listening to music, singing, hearing readings from the Bible or other writings, offering prayers, and being strengthened and encouraged by the experience. People who are drawn to corporate worship may be looking for a community where they can receive support, encouragement, and a sense of belonging. They may be looking for a community where they can use their gifts and share in a common experience, a common task. The important thing with embracing worship as a spiritual practice is to seek out a community where you are comfortable, a place where you are accepted and loved just as you are, a place where you can worship in the way that meets your needs and enlightens your spirit.

Yoga, Tai Chi, and other forms of movement—These spiritual practices focus on seeking harmony in mind, body, and spirit through movement. Through the use of poses, the practitioner can slow down physically and mentally, making space for the spiritual dimension of life. For some, yoga and Tai Chi are spiritual disciplines because they require repeated effort and practice intended to create harmony within the individual and with the Divine. Yoga and Tai Chi are recognized as practices for reducing stress, improving flexibility, and restoring balance. These outcomes can have a spiritual benefit because they impact the overall well-being of a person. Some people find exercise, dance, and other forms of movement to have the same spiritual benefit because when we will feel stronger and better physically, we also feel better emotionally, and this directly benefits our spiritual well-being.

There are more spiritual practices available to you than are highlighted in this chapter. Remember, the key is to explore different practices until you find the ones that meet your needs and expectations. You might find that one works well for a period of time, but then it gets boring or seems to no longer benefit you. That's okay. Simply switch to a different practice for a while. Be sure to give yourself time to get used to a practice before you decide that it won't work for you. Sometimes you just need more time or more practice to realize the benefits of a particular spiritual practice. Using spiritual practices consistently takes intentional commitment and effort. Be kind to yourself. Some days will go well; other days, not so much. There is always tomorrow.

As you develop comfort and understanding of spiritual practices and as you intentionally and consistently use these practices, the deepening presence of the Holy One will enable you to more fully accept and embrace yourself. You can learn more about these spiritual practices and others on my website: pamnorthrup.org.

Embracing acceptance of self

[1]O LORD, you have searched me and known me. [2]You know when I sit down and when I rise up; you discern my thoughts from far away. [3]You search out my path and my lying down and are acquainted with all my ways. [4]Even before a word is on my tongue, O LORD, you know it completely. [5]You hem me in, behind and before, and lay your hand upon me. [6]Such knowledge is too wonderful for me; it is so high that I cannot attain it. [7]Where can I go from your spirit? Or where can I flee from your presence? [8]If I ascend to heaven, you are there; if I make my bed in Sheol, you are there. [9]If I take the wings of the morning and settle at the farthest limits of the sea, [10]even there your hand shall lead me, and your right hand shall hold me fast. [11]If I say, "Surely the darkness shall cover me, and the light around me become night," [12]even the darkness is not dark to you; the night is as bright as the day, for

darkness is as light to you. [13]*For it was you who formed my inward parts; you knit me together in my mother's womb.* [14]*I praise you, for I am fearfully and wonderfully made (Psalm 139).*

I am 5 feet tall and might get a little taller if I intentionally stand straighter. I've struggled with my weight my whole life and have lost and regained lots of pounds over and over again. My Dad gave me a t-shirt when I was growing up with the slogan "I'm not overweight, I'm just six inches too short." I know my Dad meant well, and at times I could laugh about that t-shirt, but it only drew attention to my perceived flaws. Now, every time I go to the doctor, I hear that I need to lose weight to be healthier. Each time I hear that I need to lose weight, I am reminded again of my flaws and feel less like the person everyone expects me to be.

Living as an overweight individual has caused me to be self-conscious around other people. I feel shame and insecurity in some situations and find that I'm always comparing myself to others. This isn't a healthy way to be in the world. Over this past year, I have been working on accepting myself just the way I am. I'll never be a tall and thin individual and that's okay with me, so I thank God every day for making me who I am.

Accepting and embracing yourself may be one of the hardest things that we do in this life. We are bombarded by messages that we are not good enough, not pretty enough, not strong enough, not smart enough, not thin enough, not tall enough.

We're told that we don't come from the "right" neighborhood" or that our education is not from the "right" schools. We're told that we are flawed because our family didn't or doesn't look "right." We're told that our ethnicity, racial heritage, or sexual identity keeps us from being accepted, respected, and honored. We're told that we're not Christian enough, or Jewish enough, or Muslim enough, or spiritual enough.

Combating these hurtful messages, whether spoken or unspoken, can be a constant battle within us and have a lasting impact on our self-acceptance and our relationships with the Divine and with others.

Beloved, you are wonderfully made by the Creator and this Creator didn't make any mistakes in creating you! And because you are God's very good creation, God wants you to accept yourself just as God accepts you!

Embracing yourself is about intentionally rejecting these hurtful messages. It's about claiming and asserting your uniqueness and individuality which makes you, you.

You are an amazing individual! You are worthy of love, respect, and honor just as you are. You have intellect, emotions, and personality that inform how you relate to life. Your unique experiences, gifts, skills, passions, talents, hopes, dreams, and aspirations set you apart from everyone else. Once you accept yourself and your unique gifts, you are set free to be who God made you to be.

God doesn't expect you to change who you are in order to be loved by the Divine. Instead, God wants you to be the best you that you can be. There is no doubt that you will face hardships and challenges in life, we all do. God never promises that life will be easy for any of us. Instead, the Holy One promises to be present with you.

Jesus said, "And remember, I am with you always, to the end of the age" (Matthew 28:2).

The prophet Isaiah speaks the word of the Lord:

> *10Do not fear, for I am with you, do not be afraid, for I am your God; I will strengthen you, I will help you, I will uphold you with my victorious right hand (Isaiah 41).*

You live in the gracious and steadfast love of the Holy One right now. It's a love that is extravagant, encompassing, and empowering. It's intended to set you free from the negative messages that hold you hostage to fear, doubt, worry, and feelings of not being enough.

God's love is a gift to you and for you so that you are comforted, strengthened, and inspired to live in love with God and others. It is also a gift for the whole of creation. No one is excluded from the net of God's love. Absolutely no one.

Beloved, may these words from Richard Rohr bring you peace and inspire you to accept yourself as God accepts you:

God loves you by becoming you, taking your side in the inner dialogue of self-accusation and defense. God loves you by turning your mistakes into grace, by constantly giving you back to yourself in a larger shape. God stands with you, and not against you, when you are tempted to shame or self-hatred. The only thing that separates you from God is the thought that you are separated from God.[33]

Embracing the acceptance of others

[1]Therefore be imitators of God, as beloved children, [2]and live in love, as Christ loved us and gave himself up for us, a fragrant offering and sacrifice to God (Ephesians 5).

Beloved, not only are we recipients of God's gift of love but we are also conveyors of that gift to others. We are called to imitate God, to abundantly share love with all those we encounter in life: members of our family, people we enjoy being around, those we struggle to accept, our neighbors and

---

[33] Richard Rohr, The Universal Christ: How a Forgotten Reality Can Change Everything We See, Hope For, and Believe, (New York: Convergent Books, 2019), 79-80.

strangers on the street, the cashier at the grocery store, the teller at the bank, the server at the restaurant, the coworker who is challenging to be around, and the person who has hurt us in some way.

This doesn't mean that they must become our best friends, that we need to set aside our hurt, or that we even need to like them. Instead, by responding to others in love, we remind them that they too have received this extravagant, encompassing, and extravagant love of the Divine that is a gift to them just as it is to us, and that it is a gift for them, just as it is for us, and the whole human family.

We live in and share this love with others, not to earn favor with God, not to guarantee our future place in heaven, not to gain a more respected position in church, society, or at work, not to make ourselves feel superior to others. Instead, we share this love with others because we are thankful for what we've received and want others to experience the gift of God's love through us.

We also need to share this love with others as Paul describes below:

> [9]*Let love be genuine; hate what is evil, hold fast to what is good;* [10]*love one another with mutual affection; outdo one another in showing honor.* [11]*Do not lag in zeal, be ardent in spirit, serve the Lord.* [12]*Rejoice in hope, be patient in suffering, persevere in prayer.* [13]*Contribute to the needs of the saints; extend hospitality to*

strangers.[14]*Bless those who persecute you; bless and do not curse them.* [15]*Rejoice with those who rejoice, weep with those who weep.* [16]*Live in harmony with one another; do not be haughty but associate with the lowly; do not claim to be wiser than you are.* [17]*Do not repay anyone evil for evil but take thought for what is noble in the sight of all.* [18]*If it is possible, so far as it depends on you, live peaceably with all (Romans 12).*

This isn't easy, nor is it meant to be. Living in the love of God sometimes means that we need to make sacrifices on behalf of others and sacrifices on behalf of creation. We can't always have things the way we want because that might harm another person. We can't always be the one in charge because life is not all about us. Living in the love of God is about valuing the other, it's about being attentive and responsive to those in need, it's about going out of your way to lift people up and encourage them in their walk of life. We need to tend to creation because that is what sustains our life in the here and now. We need to tend to our relationships with others so we can come together for the good of all.

Summary

Because of God's love for us, we are set free to live our lives to the fullest; to embrace our unique gifts, skills, and passions; to take risks and make mistakes; to try new things and cultivate new opportunities; to love who we want to love and be who we want to be without fear and anxiety. Living in the gift of God's love includes living with intention, humility, and balance. This three-fold way of living enables us to embrace paradox, mystery, and spiritual practices that nourish us as well as embracing ourselves and others. Together, these attitudes and practices give us a deeper sense of purpose, understanding, and compassion as we engage in our work and in our play and in our relationships with family, friends, co-workers, neighbors, and the Divine.

Questions to ponder

- How does living with intention, humility, and balance shape your life?

- What challenges you? What inspires you?

- How does embracing paradox, mystery, spiritual practices that nourish you, and yourself and others shape your life?

- What challenges you? What inspires you?

- How can you engage living with intention, humility, and balance more fully in your life?

- How can you engage embracing paradox, mystery, spiritual practices, and accepting yourself and others more fully in your life?

CHAPTER 12

Summary of Part Two—Revealing the Certainty of God's Love

After untangling the five common knots, Part Two focused on revealing God's love that wraps you completely.

Everything about God's love is a gift. While God gives you this gift with no strings attached, God doesn't force it upon you because forced love isn't love at all. You decide what you do with it. Do you toss it aside unopened, do you put it on a shelf for a rainy day, or do you open it and allow it to make a difference in your life? Like every giver of gifts, God wants you to open the gift and receive its many blessings.

God's love is extravagant, encompassing, and empowering. Together, they are the net that will never fail you. They expand beyond your wildest imaginations to cover every aspect of what life has in store for you. They cover you with comfort when you feel pain, hope when you face despair, joy when sorrows abound, and peace when the troubles of this world threaten to overwhelm you. The extravagant, encompassing, and empowering love of God enables you to keep on living, to keep on trying, to keep on being the you God created you to be.

The attributes and blessings of God's love are acceptance, compassion, inclusion, peace, joy, comfort, strength, hope, interconnectedness, and courage. They support you on the roller coaster we call life and enable you to be the best you that you can be. They are the basis on which you can thrive in life and grow in love for one another and for the Holy One who bestows these blessings. Whether you are a person of a particular faith tradition or someone who claims no religious affiliation, these blessings are yours because of the Holy One whose expansive and abundant love covers you, me, and all of creation.

Living in the blessings of God's love is about living with intention, humility, and balance. It's about embracing paradox, mystery, and spiritual practices that nourish you. Living in the blessings of God's love enables you to embrace yourself and others. Cultivating these habits positively impacts your life and your relationships with the Holy One and each other. Together they strengthen your capacity to enjoy life and the people who share it with you. Attending to these habits, helps you experience the fullness of God's extravagant, encompassing, and empowering love. This enables you to live a more peaceful life, a life where relationships matter more than accomplishments and uniqueness matters more than conformity.

CONCLUSION

Knots are interesting to me. They are both useful and decorative. When I was a teenager, I tied knots to make beautiful macramé belts, wall hangings, and plant holders. As a Girl Scout, I tied knots to lash sticks together to make tables and other items used in camping. We use knots when tying shoelaces, bow or neckties, creating hairstyles, handling projects around the house, or when engaging in sports and other activities. Knots are essential in mathematics, science, and medicine.

Yet, knots are also problematic. They can refer to stressful situations, challenging relationships, or the way our stomach feels when we're worried about something. Knots can keep you up at night while you struggle with a tough decision you need to make or a tricky conversation you need to have. It doesn't matter what's causing a knot. Knots will quickly become a tangled mess when they are ignored.

And what a knotty, tangled mess we've made of God's love! We've complicated God's love by making it about what we do and say rather than what God does. We've held a narrow view of God which limits our ability to see the bigness of who God is and the vastness of how God can be experienced. We've over-emphasized humanity's brokenness rather than celebrating God's blessings. We've endorsed practices and theological understandings which create obstacles for people.

After untying these knots, God's fantastic quilt of love wraps around us. This love is a complete and uncompromising gift to and for us. The certainty of God's abundant love embraces every aspect of who we are. It expands beyond our understanding to include all of creation and every created being.

Beloved, you can rest in the extravagant, encompassing, and empowering love of God because God adores you. You are loved. You are worthy. God accepts you just as you are. God doesn't need or require you to do or say anything to prove your love because God has already proven God's love for you. God doesn't' wait for you to become perfect, doesn't wait for you to confess your sins, doesn't wait for you to profess your faith before falling in love with you. Instead, God takes the initiative, loves you completely, and blesses you with unconditional and steadfast love that will never fail and never be diminished.

May God's love enfold you in peace and hope today and every day.

It Matters What We Believe

Some beliefs are like walled gardens. They encourage exclusiveness, and the feeling of being especially privileged.

Other beliefs are expansive and lead the way into wider and deeper sympathies.

Some beliefs are like shadows, clouding children's days with fears of unknown calamities.

Other beliefs are like sunshine, blessing children with the warmth of happiness.

Some beliefs are divisive, separating the saved from the unsaved, friends from enemies.

Other beliefs are bonds in a world community. Where sincere differences beautify the pattern.

Some beliefs are like blinders, shutting off the power to choose one's own direction.

Other beliefs are like gateways opening wide vistas for exploration.

Some beliefs weaken a person's selfhood. They blight the growth of resourcefulness.

Other beliefs nurture self-confidence and enrich the feeling of personal worth.

Some beliefs are rigid, like the body of death, impotent in a changing world.

Other beliefs are pliable, like the young sapling, ever growing with the upward thrust of life.[34]

Sophia Lyon Falls

---

[34] Sophia Lyon Fahs, *Singing the Living Tradition*, (Boston: Unitarian Universalist Association, 1993) 657.

BIBLIOGRAPHY

Brené Brown. *The Gifts of Perfection: Let Go of Who You Think You're Supposed to Be and Embrace Who You Are.* Center City, MN: Hazelton, 2010.

Carol Kelly-Gangi, ed. *A Woman's Book of Inspiration: Quotes of Wisdom and Strength.* New York: Fall River Press, 2017.

Sue Monk Kidd. *The Dance of the Dissident Daughter: A Woman's Journey from Christian Tradition to the Sacred Feminine.* New York: HarperCollins, 1996.

C. S. Lewis. *Mere Christianity.* New York: HarperCollins, 1952, 2001.

Lifting Our Voices: Readings in the Living Tradition. Boston: The Unitarian Universalist Association, 2015.

Peter Marty. *the anatomy of grace.* Minneapolis: Augsburg Fortress, 2008.

Brennan Manning. *The Ragamuffin Gospel.* Sisters, OR: Multnomah Publishers, 1990.

Bruce Marshall. *What We Share: Collected Meditations, Volume 2.* collected and edited by Patricia Frevert, Boston: Skinner House, 2002.

Henri Nouwen. *Our Greatest Gift: A Meditation on Dying and Caring.* New York: HarperCollins, 1994.

Richard Rohr. *The Universal Christ: How a Forgotten Reality can change everything we see, hope for, and believe.* New York: Convergent, 2019.

Joyce Rupp, *Constant Hope: Reflection and Meditations to Strengthen the Spirit.* New London, CT: Twenty-third Publications, 2019.

Singing the Living Tradition. Boston: The Unitarian Universalist Association, 1993.

Rami Shapiro. *Accidental Grace: Poems, Prayers, Psalms.* Brewster, MA: Paraclete Press, 2015.

Danielle Shroyer. *Original Blessing: Putting Sin in its Rightful Place.* Minneapolis: Augsburg Fortress, 2016.

Barbara Brown Taylor. *An Altar in the World: A Geography of Faith.* New York: HarperOne, 2009.

Tullian Tchividjian. *Surprised by Grace: God's Relentless Pursuit of Rebels.* Wheaten, IL: Crossway, 2010.

Joan Tollifson. *Nothing to Grasp.* Salisbury: United Kingdom: Non-Duality Press, 2012.

Leo Tolstoy. *A Calendar of Wisdom*. Translated by Peter Sekirin. New York: Scribner, 1997.

Philip Yancy. *Disappointment with God: Three Questions No One Asks Aloud*. Grand Rapids, MI: Zondervan, 2015.

An Invitation

Are you interested in discussing this book further?

Has reading this book stirred up something inside you that you'd like to explore?

Are you troubled by an experience you had with a church or someone in a church?

Have you been wounded by organized religion?

Do you feel unloved by God?

Would you enjoy conversation about the intersection of faith and life?

Do you feel a yearning for the spiritual?

Does deepening your understanding and use of spiritual practices interest you?

Are you curious about the concept of spiritual companioning and want to learn more?

Have you always wanted to be an author, but don't know how to get started?

If you've answered yes to any of these questions or would just like to chat with me, I'd love to talk with you.

Please visit my webpage at www.pamnorthrup.org to tell me more about what interests you.

Resources for engaging spiritual practices are available on the site.

You can also email me directly at pam@pamnorthrup.org.

SELF-PUBLISHING SCHOOL

Self-Publishing School helped me, and now
I want them to help you with this FREE WEBINAR!

Discover the EXACT 3-step blueprint you need
to become a bestselling author in 3 months.

Even if you're busy, bad at writing, or don't know where
to start, you CAN write a bestseller and build your best life.

With tools and experience across a variety niches
and professions, Self-Publishing School is the only
resource you need to take your book to the finish line!

DON'T WAIT

Watch this FREE WEBINAR now, and
Say "YES" to becoming a bestseller:

https://xe172.isrefer.com/go/affegwebinar/
bookbrosinc7483/

ACKNOWLEDGMENTS

I am deeply grateful for:

My dear husband, Bob, who graciously gave me the time, space, and understanding to complete this book and who inspired me to keep on keeping on.

My family and friends who supported the effort with words of encouragement.

My initial readers for their feedback and suggestions including Laura Prill, Renee Anderson, Amanda Northrup, and Robin Kirk.

My coach, Heidi Kleine, for holding me accountable throughout the process and for providing wisdom and insight.

My collaborators for doing their part to get this book ready for publication: Katie Chambers, Beacon Point LLC, editor; Jen Henderson, Wild Words Formatting, formatter; Kevin Coppolino, book cover designer; and Abigail C. Falk, cover photography

My colleagues at Self-Publishing School for the resources to help me maneuver through the ins and outs of self-publishing. Without Self-Publishing School, I wouldn't have known how to accomplish the task of publishing this book.

ABOUT THE AUTHOR

Pam Northrup was ordained in the Evangelical Lutheran Church in America (ELCA) in 2006. She served as pastor of three congregations before becoming a hospice chaplain. Pam has been recognized as an outstanding preacher, thoughtful worship leader, engaging teacher, faithful spiritual companion, and compassionate listener.

Her passion is journeying with people as they face the ups and downs of life. And as such, she enjoys cultivating relationships with people of all ages and across all faith traditions, including those who claim no religious affiliation. She enjoys spending time with friends and family—especially her grandchildren—traveling, reading, journaling, making prayer beads, playing board games, listening to music, coloring, and making art collages.

In 2019, Pam published her first book, *On the Way: Short Stories & Biblical Reflections on Caring for a Loved One in Hospice,* in memory of her mother who died while in hospice care.

Pam lives in Knightdale, NC, with her husband, Bob, and their dog. You can read a collection of her sermons and blog posts and learn more about her at www.pamnorthrup.org.

Contact her at pam@pamnorthrup.org if you'd like to talk about spiritual companioning, speaking, preaching, and teaching opportunities.

Made in the USA
Columbia, SC
05 June 2020